SPANISH *for* GRINGOS

Shortcuts, Tips and Secrets to Successful Learning

by

William C. Harvey, MS

Illustrations by Paul Meisel

BARRON'S

For all the gringos who try...

grin-go \ ˈgrin-(ˌ) gō\ *n, pl* **gringos** [Sp, alter. of *griego* Greek, stranger, fr. L *Graecus* Greek] (1849): a foreigner in Spain or Latin America esp. when of English or American origin...

By permission. From Webster's 9th New Collegiate Dictionary © 1989 by Merriam-Webster Inc., publisher of the Merriam-Webster dictionaries.

About the Author

William C. Harvey is founder of Language Services Institute, a highly-successful conversational Spanish program aimed specifically at meeting the needs of today's busy adult learner. For the past 12 years he has taught Spanish and ESL (English as a Second Language) in school districts and community colleges, as well as in private industry. He has also traveled extensively throughout the West Coast giving workshops and seminars to teachers and professional organizations. Mr. Harvey holds a bachelor's degree in Spanish and a master's degree in Bilingual-Bicultural Education from Cal State University, Fullerton, where he received the "Project of the Year" award for his work in ESL Curriculum Development.

All inquiries should be addressed to:
Barron's Educational Series, Inc.
250 Wireless Boulevard
Hauppauge, NY 11788

International Standard Book No. 0-8120-4434-7

Library of Congress Catalog Card No. 90-1266

Library of Congress Cataloging-in-Publication Data

Harvey, William C.
    Spanish for gringos: shortcuts, tips, and secrets to successful
learning/by William C. Harvey.
        p.   cm.
    ISBN 0-8120-4434-7
    1. Spanish language—Textbooks for foreign speakers—English.
I. Title.
PC4128.H38   1990
468.2'421—dc20   90-1266
                                                          CIP

Printed in the United States of America

30 29 28 27 26 25 24 23 22 21

CONTENTS

Hola, fellow gringos!

Finally, after years of teaching classroom Spanish using the dreadful "textbook approach," I got fed up and decided to try something different. Having picked up Spanish myself by hanging around non-English speakers, I'd discovered what gringos *really* needed to learn *el español.* So I put together a series of practical, easy-to-follow shortcuts, tips, and secrets to success—designed specifically for folks who aren't interested in "studying" a foreign language. In place of traditional units and lessons, *Spanish for Gringos* is intended as a guidebook and offers nothing more than helpful suggestions. This approach should make your language learning experience easy and *muy divertido* (lots of fun)!

Adiós for now,

Bill

Reasons Why Spanish is Easy to Learn

Other languages are great, but believe me—I've chosen Spanish because it is the easiest of them all. I've spent my life developing *Spanish for Gringos* for six very good reasons.

1   Spanish is a lot like English.

Most Spanish words have the same Latin-based form as their English equivalents. Many words in both languages look and sound almost the same, which makes guessing a breeze.

2   Spanish is not complicated.

Conversations in Spanish can be kept short and sweet. Complex messages are often exchanged using only a few simple words. Only an understanding of basic grammar and pronunciation patterns is needed for successful communication to take place.

3   It's OK if you blow it.

Spanish speakers enjoy helping gringos who try. Hispanics are proud, warm-hearted people who admire those with a sincere interest in learning their native tongue. So cheer up. Lousy Spanish only makes *you* feel stupid.

4   Spanish is not hard to practice.

All across the nation, the Hispanic population continues to grow at a tremendous rate. Regular exposure to Spanish should not be a major problem. Neither should it be difficult for the learner to find someone to "practice with." Also remember that lots of Spanish still lies just south of the border.

5   Spanish can be profitable.

American business people have recently discovered that buying and selling in more than one language makes good business sense. And with Hispanics in the United States now spending millions a day, their market has become a primary target of corporate America. Increasingly, companies are providing Spanish training for employees. And better pay seems to make learning that much easier. So revise that résumé! Learning Spanish can lead to financial success.

6   Spanish is fun to learn.

There's nothing like the thrill of speaking Spanish and being understood for the first time. Or the *second* time. It's not long before gringos get "hooked." Maybe it's because communication in a new language allows you to meet, understand, and assist more people. That does wonders for the self-image. Spanish also can make life more fun. In traveling to Spanish-speaking countries, common activities such as shopping and dining suddenly become more enjoyable and exciting. A second language is like a new toy—so play with it! After mastering Spanish you will find that similar languages, like French and Italian, are easier to learn. And don't worry about staying motivated. It seems that once gringos get rolling in *español,* they're usually very difficult to stop!

"Who Needs It?"

Spanish for Gringos is not *for everyone.*

For those of you who plan on living in Spain or Latin America and need extensive language training...I'm sorry. And to those who already speak Spanish and are looking to improve their reading and writing skills...I apologize. You see, this guidebook was *not* written for people whose intentions are to "study."

Spanish for Gringos is for everybody else.

Most of what you'll find here is basic, practical information that you can use right away, with a lot of the technical "stuff" trimmed away. Generalizations about Spanish are made. Translations are not "precise." And the primary theme is to *assist gringos only,* as they begin communication with Spanish speakers at work or at play.

Although this guidebook should help any Spanish learners, it is basically *an orientation to the type of Spanish that is commonly spoken here in the United States.*

Before You Begin

OK, *brace yourselves!* This guidebook contains *no* drills, *no* exercises, *no* worksheets, and *no* tests!

...Instead, learners will be asked to follow some RATHER UNUSUAL GUIDELINES

- **Forget what you've been told!** (You'll just get hung-up on useless details.) There's no such thing as perfect Spanish, so don't get stuck trying to figure out the best way to say something. This book gives you only what you *need* to know. Instead of traditional grammar and pronunciation practice, try the practical shortcuts, tips, and secrets to success. If you follow the useful suggestions, you'll be all right most of the time.

- **Spend most of your time listening!** (You'll be talking in no time.) To learn the way a baby learns language, it's important to "take in" lots of Spanish at the beginning. Listen to fluent speakers. Soon, new words will emerge naturally in everyday conversation. Use the one-liners and greetings freely, but don't force speech until you feel ready to speak. Language tapes can be helpful. But real-life practice is better!

- **Act as if you know more than you do!** (You'll soon believe that you *are* fluent.) Learn to have self-confidence around people who speak only Spanish. Even if you don't understand a word, smile and laugh a lot. "Concentrate" when you are asked a question, and always answer with a short response. Imitate verbal and nonverbal expressions. Be assertive, yet remain friendly. Experiment with new words and phrases. Fake it, and you'll be speaking Spanish *pronto!*

- **Don't make excuses!** (You'll never get started if you do.) Recent studies* have shown the following statements about language learning to be *Untrue!*

You need to do grammar exercises . . . . *No!*
You need to develop good pronunciation . . . . *No!*
You need to start at an early age . . . . *No!*
You need to memorize vocabulary lists . . . . *No!*
You need to be "good at languages" . . . . *No!*

So there! The truth is you have *no excuse* and...
You *will* learn Spanish quickly and easily . . . . *Sí!*

- **Most of all, relax!** The idea of learning a new language scares the life out of most people, so don't feel ashamed. Just accept the fact that you're going to sound strange and look awkward for a while. It's no big deal. This guidebook is designed to relieve you of stress and frustration. Never give up! Don't worry about a thing, have some fun, and just go for it. With *Spanish for Gringos* learning *no es problema.*

Checklist
1 **Comfortable chair** ☐
2 **Background music** ☐
3 **Favorite beverage** ☐
4 **Laid-back attitude** ☐

*Dulay, Heidi. *Language Two*. New York: Oxford University Press, 1982; Krashen, Stephen D. and Terrell, Tracy D. *The Natural Approach*. Hayward, California: The Alemany Press, 1983.

1

CHAPTER *UNO*

¿Habla español?

(Do You Speak Spanish?)

Spanish Words Most Gringos Already Know:

americano	*cerveza*
amigo	*margarita*
amor	*tequila*
español	*vino*
Julio Iglesias	
loco	*bueno*
macho	*grande*
padre	*mucho*
plaza	*más*
pueblo	
rancho	*adiós*
señor	*gracias*
señorita	*Feliz Navidad*
	hasta la vista
fiesta	*por favor*
cha-cha-cha	*pronto*
La Bamba	*sí*
olé	
	dinero
burrito	*uno*
chile	*dos*
enchilada	*tres*
salsa	
taco	

Spanglish

A unique blend of Spanish and English has gradually evolved in the United States as more and more Spanish speakers and English speakers have made attempts to communicate. Nationwide, Spanglish is alive and well (though words may vary from region to region). You see, many English words either can't be exactly translated into Spanish or are just easier to say when mixed with English. What's great is that they all sound like words gringos know. Check out these easy-to-remember "Spanish Englishisms":

NOTE
Spanglish is not street slang! But it's *not Spanish,* either. So some people may make comments. Be prepared!

SPANGLISH	ENGLISH	SPANISH
bloquear	to block	*obstruir*
cachar	to catch	*coger*
chequear	to check	*revisar*
cuitiar	to quit	*renunciar*
mistear	to miss	*faltar*
parquear	to park	*estacionar*
pichar	to pitch	*lanzar*
puchar	to push	*empujar*
taipiar	to type	*escribir a máquina*
tochar	to touch	*tocar*
trostear	to trust	*confiar*
wachar	to watch	*mirar*

Did you know? Mixing both languages when "you can't remember" is still OK!

HOT TIP!

If it's close—they'll probably get it! Since Spanglish and English are so similar, you really don't need to worry about pronunciation.

SPANGLISH	ENGLISH	SPANISH
la baika	bike	*la bicicleta*
las brekas	brakes	*los frenos*
la carpeta	carpet	*la alfombra*
el cauche	couch	*el sofá*
la factoria	factory	*la fábrica*
el lonche	lunch	*el almuerzo*
la marqueta	market	*el mercado*
el mofle	muffler	*el silenciador*
el pay	pie	*el pastel*
el raite	ride	*un paseo*
la troca	truck	*el camión*
la yarda	yard	*el patio*

NOTE
Don't struggle with the pronunciation of Spanish words yet! You'll be getting the "Secrets to Soundmaking" shortly.

Check these out! English words used as Spanglish that can even be pronounced exactly like English:

el bar	el income tax	el rock-n-roll
el breaktime	el manager	el six-pack
el cash	la microwave	el show
el cassette	la movie	el stress
el closet	el nightclub	el supermarket
la dishwasher	el overtime	el teenager
el folder	la party	el time-out
el freeway	el pitcher	la TV
el golf	la pizza	el VCR
el hockey	el record	el windshield wiper

la IBM	los Levis
el Hilton	el Kleenex

HOT TIP!
Are you aware that names of people, cities, streets, buildings, companies, and brand names are *not* usually translated into Spanish?

Vamos a Chicago.   We go to Chicago.
El señor John Candy habla español.   Mister John Candy speaks Spanish.
Trabajo en el Hilton.   I work at the Hilton.

Understanding
Spanish Speakers

You're right. It does sound like one long word. Everything is too fast.
So what's a gringo to do? Well, don't panic. Relax, smile, and try these
Five Secrets to Success:

1 Focus on the message.

Listen for key words and how they're expressed, instead of trying
to understand *the whole enchilada.* Are they asking or telling you
something? Avoid translating each word. Concentrate on the
main idea only.

2 Use your hands and face.

Express comprehension by pointing, moving, or touching things.
Make faces. Write or draw what you think they're trying to say. Be
aggressive, yet friendly. Soon, they'll get into the act. Laugh
together and there will be *no problema.*

3 Say: *Más despacio, por favor.*

(Mahs des·pah'syo, por fah·bo'r) which means: "More slowly
please." Or say *¿Qué?* (kay) and *¿Cómo?* (ko'mo) which mean
"What?" and "How's that?"

4 Listen for the English.

Since both languages are Latin based, many Spanish words sound
a lot like English. Guess and you'll probably be right!

5 Relax and try again.

Swallow your pride and remember—they're having as much
trouble as you are. Lighten up, believe in yourself, and *español*
will begin to make sense.

Hey, Listen! (¡Escuche!)

Don't say a word! You don't have to. Much like children learn their native tongue, it's best to *listen first!* So don't force yourself to speak. After listening to Spanish for a while, *it will gradually start coming out of you!* For now, try some of these easy (and inexpensive) ways to pick up on those new "foreign noises":

- Listen to Spanish radio stations (check local listings).
- Find out which TV stations also air in Spanish.
- Rent Spanish movies on videocassette.
- Buy Spanish music tapes and CDs.
- Ride city buses or subways through Spanish-speaking areas.
- See a Spanish language play or musical performance.
- Attend a Spanish-speaking religious service of your faith.
- Join a Spanish-speaking club, team, or organization.
- Check into travel packages to Spain or Latin America.
- Befriend those Spanish speakers whom you see regularly.
- Take a Spanish class or buy a workbook with tapes.

HOT TIP!

You can obviously add your own ideas to this list. But however you choose to *escuchar* (listen), always remember the three **C**s: **C**alm down, Observe **C**losely, and **C**oncentrate on what's being said!

The "Nonverbals"

Guess what? If you'd like to communicate in Spanish, but don't feel like speaking, there's an easy and fun way to send messages. As with most cultures, certain *hand signals, facial expressions,* and *body language* convey valuable meaning. Here are some of my favorite hand signals from Mexico.

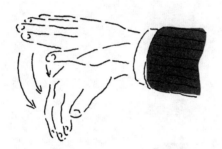

I love it! Talk without speaking!

Venga.
Come here.

By moving your hand (or arm) in a downward motion, you're calling someone to you.

Un momento.
Just a moment.

By putting your thumb and index finger together, you're telling someone, "Hold on just a moment. I'll be right with you."

No gracias.
No thanks.

By moving your pointer finger back and forth, you're telling someone "No" or "Don't."

More Nonverbals

Touching your elbow while looking at folks is the same as calling them tightwads or "cheap."

NOTE
If you know how to say the words, add them for emphasis.

Pointing to your eye means "Be careful" or "Watch out!"

Always point upwards, with palm side of the hand toward you, when referring to the height of a person...

...and outwards, palm-side-down, when referring to the height of an object or animals.

NOTE
There are many more, so take time to observe people as they interact. Ask the meanings if you're not sure. Practice the nonverbals and you'll be able to "communicate" right away!

2

CHAPTER *DOS*

Las primeras palabras

(The First Words)

Secrets to Soundmaking

Basically, you need to know only *five* primary Spanish sounds that will make you comprehensible and help you to understand more. When speaking Spanish, if you make the following sounds every time the corresponding letter appears, you'll sound just like a native speaker. When? *Every time the letter appears!* Try making these sounds toward the front of your mouth instead of the back—with little or no air coming out. Short choppy sounds are better than long stretched-out ones. Go ahead, practice now that nobody's listening and soon you will be able to impress your friends.

Trust me! Know these and you will be on your way!

a (ah) like y**a**cht
e (eh) like m**e**t
i (ee) like k**ee**p
o (oh) like **o**pen
u (oo) like sp**oo**n

HOT TIP!

Exactness doesn't matter! As I said before—if it's close, they'll probably get it. Besides, the goal of this guidebook is getting people to communicate, *not* teaching all the different Spanish sounds. So stop fretting. You sound great to me!

The Big Five

a *banana, Panamá, La Bamba, cha-cha-cha*
e *tres, excelente, olé, elefante, Pelé*
i *sí, dividir, Trini, Sandinista, Miami*
o *loco, ocho, no, Colorado, dos*
u *Lulú, mucho, tú, burro, Uruguay*

HOT TIPS!

- These 8 are the only "toughies." The rest can be pronounced the *same as English!*
- Take note! Gringos have the most trouble with *qu*.

The "Others"

Easy enough. But what about the *other* sounds in Spanish? Good news—they're not much different from English. But here are a few that may cause confusion.

g has two sounds: **g**[1] (g) like **g**o and **g**[2] (h) like **h**ello, when followed by **e** or **i**.
h (*Don't* pronounce it; like **k** in knife.)
j (h)   like **h**ot
ll (y)   like **y**es
ñ (ny) like ca**ny**on
qu (k) like **k**iss
v (b)   like **b**reak
z (s)   like **s**it

More volume!
I can't hear you.

- Like the Big Five, these sounds have *no exceptions!* In Spanish, respective sounds are always the same *every time their corresponding letter appears!*
- Don't worry about your "regional accent." Making yourself understood in Spanish doesn't depend on what part of the United States *you* are from.

Now, let's try to put all these "pieces of noise" together. Refer back to the Secrets to Soundmaking as you read the following **(ALOUD)**:

g^1	*gorila, garaje, guacamole, Paraguay*
g^2	*general, Geraldo, gimnasio, rígido*
h	*huevo, hombre, hola, ahora*
j	*Juan, trabajo, frijoles, Julio*
ll	*llama, millón, tortillas, amarillo*
ñ	*señor, mañana, español, piña colada*
qu	*poquito, qué pasa, tequila, quesadilla*
v	*vino, Victoria, viva, hasta la vista*
z	*López, cerveza, Venezuela, González*

HOT TIPS!

- Always try to "visualize" Spanish words because they're spelled exactly as you say them. And **don't worry about what you sound like!**
- **Run 'em together...** What's really nice about the *español* is that it's put together in little pieces—just like the *inglés.* So, to sound like a native speaker, **thefasterthebetter!**
- **Read 'em Right!** By now, you've probably noticed the little accent mark (´) on parts of certain words. Don't get nervous. It only means that you're supposed to say that part of the word **LOUDER!**

*Ma-**rí**-a*

Forget about the accent mark on little words, like *sí* or *qué!* That's just how they're spelled!

Embarrassed? Then go somewhere private and shut the door!

¡ANUNCIO IMPORTANTE!

Once you become familiar with the different Spanish sounds you'll make the *first giant step toward fluency!* So why not go back and read it again!

Más Pronunciation Details!

- If there's *no* accent mark, say the *last part* of the word louder (espa**ñol**).
- For words ending in the Big Five, *n* or *s,* the *second to the last* part of the word is emphasized (enchi**la**da).
- With **rr,** roll your Rs—but *only* if you can. They'll understand if you use **r** instead.
- The **c** = "s," after *e* or *i.*
- The **d** sometimes sounds like our "th" (as in "this") in the middle and at the end of words.
- People from Spanish-speaking countries don't all sound alike, but they all understand one another and will understand you.
- Forget "rules." They'll only make it worse!

> **NOTE**
> You won't find any more pronunciation "guides" next to words in this book. Instead, learn the "Secrets to Soundmaking" and practice in "real-life" situations!

Spanish Words That Don't Need Translating

There are literally thousands of Spanish words that are easy to understand. All you have to do is focus on **the English within.** No need to translate these:

EASY

aplicación	*fotografía*	*persona*
béisbol	*importancia*	*policía*
café	*inteligente*	*posesión*
comercial	*interesante*	*posible*
conversación	*limón*	*refrigerador*
escuela	*millonario*	*teléfono*
especial	*minuto*	*televisión*
estúpido	*momento*	*turismo*
familia	*nervioso*	*universidad*
fantástico	*noviembre*	*vacación*
favorito	*operación*	*vocabularío*

The **EASIEST**

banana	*hockey*	*natural*
chocolate	*horrible*	*plaza*
color	*hospital*	*popular*
doctor	*hotel*	*radio*
final	*idea*	*taxi*
golf	*individual*	*terror*

Other Easy to Remember Words

diccionario	*instrumento*	*programa*
dieta	*moderno*	*presidente*
dólar	*música*	*reservación*
eléctrico	*producto*	*sincero*
elegante	*profesional*	*violento*
información		

Mi buena memoria (My good memory)

Start today! Make a *lista* of Spanish words (without looking back) that you already have "picked up." You'll be surprised.

_____

_____

_____

_____

_____

_____

_____

_____

¡UNA NOTICIA IMPORTANTE!
"Add" an upside-down mark in front of
¡Exclamations! and *¿Questions?*
¿Comprende?

HOT TIPS!

- **Remember:** *No pain-no gain!* As in all stretching exercises, when you pronounce this stuff, *make it hurt! Use those "mouth muscles"!*
- **Spanish sounds a bit like English—** but with an accent!
- **Be careful!** Some Spanish words look like English—but aren't. For example, *contestar* (to answer) has nothing to do with contests. And *pan* (bread) or *pie* (foot) could cause confusion!

Speak Up! (¡Hable!)

Muchos Ways to Practicar

Listening to Spanish was no big deal. The next step, then, is to practice *saying* something. (Once you've warmed up with Spanish words that resemble English, try these practice techniques for improving pronunciation, while picking up the hard-to-remember stuff:)

- Next time you're at an Hispanic restaurant, order food for everyone at the table.
- Look up and read all the names under González in the phone book. Then do the same with Sánchez or García.
- Travel through Spanish-speaking sections of town and say aloud the words on billboards and store windows. (You may get funny looks!)
- Randomly open books on the Southwest, Latin America, or Spain, and try pronouncing all the Spanish words you find.
- Next time you're alone, try reading English aloud—but use the Spanish Secrets to Soundmaking! Don't laugh—it works!
- Start slowly. Try practicing *one sound a week*!
- Tape yourself regularly while reading Spanish language newspapers or magazines.
- If possible, buy some language tapes and work with them.

HOT TIP!

The best way to learn a new language is to talk face to face with someone. Think of convenient ways to learn Spanish from Hispanic people. One popular method is to offer a little English instruction in return.

Baby's First *Palabras* (Words)

We've already taken a look at *Words Gringos Already Know* and *Should Know.* Now it's time to try words and phrases you *have to know.* In the same way a baby learns "survival words" at first, it's best to start with the Spanish that will take you the farthest. The following seem to be the words acquired first in any language. Use them to communicate complete messages. (**Wait!** Check back on the Secrets to Soundmaking!)

Hola.

agua   water
amigo   friend
baño   bathroom
bueno   good
carro   car
casa   house
comida   food
dinero   money
grande   big
hombre   man
más   more
mucho   a lot
mujer   woman
muy bien   very well
niño   child
nombre   name
número   number
persona   person
teléfono   phone
trabajo   work
por favor   please
gracias   thanks
hola   Hi!
adiós   Bye!

Put two or more together!
y = and
o = or
pero = but

These words are grasped early also: *Señor (Sr.)* is a "Mr."; *Señora (Sra.)* is a "Mrs."; *Señorita (Srta.)* is a "Miss." *Sorry,* there is no word for "Ms."—**yet**!

HOT TIPS!

Before we go on, here are a few helpful suggestions on how to use these first *palabras.*

- Do speak in "broken" Spanish, by putting only key words together. Just "mumble" the less important stuff. (We'll learn more about this later!)
- If you can't remember a word, try another way to explain yourself.
- Try out *one word a day* and build from there. Gain confidence by starting off with those you like best.
- Develop a system for remembering. Play "word–picture" association games.
- Let others correct you. It's OK! Natural mistakes help you learn faster.
- For words you use a lot, it might be a good idea to learn others that mean the same thing.
- Don't forget that dialects may vary. You're going to encounter *muchas más palabras* that won't be mentioned here!

(So, how's your soundmaking?)

My Favorite First Words

Here are more gems that work all by themselves.

ahora mismo or *ahorita*   right now
después afterwards
antes before
mientras during
entonces   then
ya already
demasiado   too much
otra another
otra vez   again
casi almost
juntos   together
solo alone
todo   all of it

los demás   the rest of them
ninguno   none of them
cualquiera   any of them
cada uno   each one
ambos   both of them
algunos   some
varios   several
nada   nothing
siguiente   the next one
mismo   the same
diferente   different
primero   first
último   last

The Greetings and Stuff

Having any problems in getting started? Your troubles are over. Memorize these as one long word and they'll think you're fluent!

Buenos días.   Good morning

Buenas tardes.   Good afternoon

Buenas noches.   Good evening or Good night

HOT TIPS!

- To really impress, just greet with: *¡Buenos!* (daytime) or *¡Buenas!* (late afternoon and evening) *¡Hola!* Hi! and *¡Qué tal!* How's it going! can be used anytime.

- Instead of *Adiós* (Good-bye), try *Nos vemos* (we'll see ya), or

  luego (later)
  Hasta mañana (Until) (tomorrow)
  la vista (next time)

- Find some more and have fun!

More Courtesies

"Hello?"

¿Aló?, ¿Bueno? or *¿Diga?* are all good when you answer the phone. "Who's calling?" is *¿De parte de quién?*

"Who's There?"

When you knock and want to enter, it's *¿Se puede?* (Can I come in?). To say "Come in!" use: *¡Pase!* or *¡Adelante!*

"Thanks!"

Instead of the old, *Muchas gracias* for "Thanks a lot," try these stronger words of appreciation: ***¡Muchísimas gracias! ¡Mil gracias!*** or the one I use: ***¡Muy amable!***

Por favor is "please."
De nada is "you're welcome."
Lo siento is "I'm sorry."

> Remember that Spanish speakers exchange greetings regularly. Try learning other ways folks say hello, and don't be afraid to "greet" someone back!

"Excuse Me!"

Whenever you'd like to get through a crowd, use *¡Con permiso!* If you cough or sneeze, say: *¡Perdón!* To get someone's attention, try: *¡Disculpe! ¡Pase!* is "Go ahead!" *¡Salud!* is "Bless you!"

así aou – soso

¿Qué pasa?   vs.   ¿Cómo está usted?

¿Qué pasa?
This is the standard "What's happening?" Sometimes you'll be greeted with *¿Qué*...(and something else.)? Don't worry! They're still only asking what's going on. Here's the easy way out: always answer with— *"¡Sin novedad!"* or *"¡Nada!"* (Nothing new!)

¿Cómo está usted?
Everyone knows this one. It means, "How are you?" And as with *¿Qué pasa?*, when you hear, *¿Cómo*...(something)? you can "sneak by" using the classic, *¡Muy bien!* (Just fine!)

> **NOTE**
> Later on, we'll take a look at other ways to answer these *¿Qué...?* and *¿Cómo...?* questions.

Las presentaciones
(Introductions)

There are many ways to say, "Nice to meet you!" but the most common is *¡Mucho gusto!* During the introduction, don't forget to shake the other person's hand. If something is said to *you* first, smile and say, *¡igualmente!,* which translates to, "Same to you."

¿Cómo se llama? (What's your name?) and *Me llamo* _____. (My name is _____). are also nice to know!

HOT TIPS!

- *¿Y usted?* means, "And you?"
- *¿Qué pasó?* is "What's the matter?" or "What happened?"
- And mind your manners!

¿Dónde está?
(Where is it?)

More than likely, the very first question you'll get asked will be, "Where's the bathroom?" (Whenever anyone needs directions, they'll use, *¿Dónde está...?*) Here, then, is what you'll need:

...*a la derecha* = to the right

...*a la izquierda* = to the left

...*adelante* or *derecho* = straight ahead

...*aquí* or *acá* = here

...*ahí* = there

...*allá* = over there

NOTE
Watch and listen for *está!* See if you can guess how it's used.

¡Viva el vocabulario!

Following are three groups of words most folks seem to pick up and use almost immediately.

Los números
(The numbers)

0   *cero*
1   *uno*
2   *dos*
3   *tres*
4   *cuatro*
5   *cinco*
6   *seis*
7   *siete*
8   *ocho*
9   *nueve*

Los colores
(The colors)

black   *negro*
blue   *azul*   azules – blue
brown   *pardo* or *café* (Mexico)   Marrón
gray   *gris*
green   *verde*
orange   *anaranjado*
purple   *morado*
red   *rojo*
white   *blanco*
yellow   *amarillo*

La clase
(The class)

en = on

el libro

el lápiz

la pluma

el papel

el cuaderno

la mesa

el pizarrón   blackboard

la tiza or
el gis

el escritorio

la silla

HOT TIPS!

- More numbers will be introduced later. Can you say the preceding numbers with your eyes closed?

- "Look up" more colors if you need others. And learn by "word–picture association." For example, *BLANK* white paper is *blanco*. (How clever can you be?)

- More new words are on their way. For now, go find these things around you. Touch them and name them in *español*—and no cheating!

CHOOSE 'n USE   Here are some sentences that will help you put these words to practice. Fill in the blanks, read each sentence aloud, and plan ways to use them in real-life situations.

• Los números

Mi número de teléfono es...   My telephone number is... (542-8763, etc.).

¿Dónde está el cuarto número...?   Where's room number... (five, three, etc.)?

• Los colores

Me gusta el color...   I like the color...(purple, red, etc.).
¿Es...o...? Is it...(black, etc.) or...(white, etc.)?
Hay algunos del color...   There are some...(orange, etc.) ones.

• La clase

¿Tiene usted un/una...   Do you have a...(pen, book, etc.)?
...está en... The...(pen, notebook, etc.) is "in, on, or at" the...(desk, table etc.).
Necesito...   I need the...(pen, chair, etc.).

At the end of this book you'll discover a Personal Success Chart. Use it! Simply pencil in your "experiences." Try out your new skills regularly. See how fast your **lista** can grow!

3

CHAPTER *TRES*
Más, Más, Más
(More, More, More)

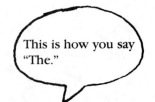

This is how you say "The."

The *El* and *La* Business

If you want to name a single object or person, put either *el* (masculine) or *la* (feminine) in front. It may seem strange, but as you continue to learn more *español,* you will need to know the meanings of "masculine" and "feminine." In Spanish, single objects require either an *el* or a *la* in front. This has nothing to do with an object's sex! It's just the *el* and *la* Business! In order to remember which one to use, just check to see if the word ends in either an *o* (generally masculine) or an *a* (generally feminine).

el

el taco
el amigo
el burro

el gato
el perro

la

la enchilada
la señorita
la cucaracha

HOT TIPS!

- A few words are weird **(i.e., *el sofá, la mano, el problema*).**
- Some words don't end in **o** or **a** (i.e., *el elefante, la paz*)
- *El* and *la* refer not only to male and female persons **(i.e., *el señor, la dama*),** but to animals as well.
- *It doesn't matter* if you get confused and use the wrong one, *you'll still be understood!* So don't hold back!

More *El/La* Business and *Un/Una*

The following are common questions and answers about one part of Spanish that is completely foreign to English.

1 Can *el* and *la* also refer to more than one person, animal or thing?
No way, José. Two or more *tacos* and *enchiladas* become:
los *tacos* and **las** *enchiladas*

> Notice what happens to *el.*
> More than *uno* is *los.*
>
> See? You've got to tag on the "s" at the end.

2 How do I say "a" or "an" instead of "the"?
At times in English we use "a" or "an" to say "any old thing." In Spanish, use **un** or **una**:
un *taco* and **una** *enchilada* are "a" taco and "an" enchilada.

> And guess what? **Unos** and **unas** mean "some."

3 Why is this aspect of Spanish a little confusing?
The answer is simple: You're not used to it yet! Grasping these concepts may take a little time. Besides, your messing up Spanish won't make much difference! Your listeners will figure out what you said anyway. But if you do "get corrected" just say to yourself—"I'll get it right the next time!"

HOT TIPS!

- Words (naming things, people, or concepts) that have the following endings, need *la* (feminine) in front.
  = *a*
  = *sión*
  = *tad*
  = *ción*
  = *dad*
  = *umbre*
  = *ambre*
  Other word endings take *el* (masculine).
- Textbooks call this *masculine* and *feminine gender.*
- By the way, *él*, with an accent mark means "he."
- *Un/una* is "a/an" and *uno* is "one."
- Talking about "more than one" (plurals) is a lot like *inglés*:
  cuatro tacos
  four tacos
  cinco relojes
  five watches

The Once-and-for-All Rule

HOT TIPS!

- You can expect to get the hang of this *rápido!*
- Matching the **o**'s and **a**'s works great with *"Los colores"*!: *Much**os** carr**os** blanc**os*** Many white cars; *much**as** cas**as** blanc**as**.* **But:** *much**os** carr**os** azul**es***

As we've learned, talking about "more than one" (plural) in Spanish is very much as it is in English; (**un** *taco* → **dos** *tacos*). Words not ending in the Big Five take **es** at the end; **un** *doctor* → **dos** *doctor**es***).

What isn't like English is what I call the "Once-and-for-all Rule." You see, not only do all Spanish words that name (nouns) or describe (adjectives) things, people, or concepts need "s," or "es" to make them plural, but when they are used together, the **o**'s and **a**'s (masculine and feminine) must match.

*Much**os** tacos*   Many tacos
y and
*Much**as** enchilad**as***   Many enchiladas

NOTA IMPORTANTE

Muchos means "many."
Mucho means "a great deal" or "a lot."...And don't confuse *mucho* with *muy*, which means "very."

...**y**...

*poc**o*** a little bit   *poqu**ito*** a very little bit
*poc**os*** a few   *poqu**itos*** very few

Did you notice?
= *ito* and = *ita* word endings reduce things.

The "One-a-Day" One-liners

A very good way to gain confidence while learning a new language is to speak in short, meaningful phrases. Instead of struggling with the formation of correct long sentences, expressive one-liners can be used—especially when there's really nothing left to say. And using them will make you feel more confident! You'll sound more fluent than you actually are. Practice a new one every day...(Careful! They're addictive!)

Use these phrases whenever you think it might be appropriate.

Por supuesto.   Of course!

¿Es verdad? or *¿De veras?*   Really?

Quizás.   Maybe!

Me alegro.   I'm so glad!

Es verdad.   That's the truth!

Más o menos.   More or less!

¿Está bien?   Is that OK?

Está bien.   That's OK!

Creo que sí.   I think so!

¡Cómo no!   Why not!

¿Es posible?   Is it possible?

Es posible.   It's possible!

¡Claro!   Sure!

¿De acuerdo?   Agreed?

De acuerdo.   I agree!

¡Sin duda!   No doubt!

Depende.   That depends!

A lo contrario.   On the contrary; just the opposite.

For Busy *Personas*

¡Ya me voy!   I'm leaving now!

¡Ya se fue!   He or she has left!

¡Ahora vengo!   I'll be right back!

¡Ahí viene!   Here he or she comes!

¿Listo?   Ready?

Buena idea.   Good idea!

Yo también.   Me, too!

Yo tampoco.   Me, neither!

¡Ojalá!   I hope so!

Ya veo.   I see!

¿Quién sabe?   Who knows?

¿Está seguro(a)?   Are you [he/she] sure?

¿Así?   Like this?

Lo que (usted) quiera.   Whatever you want!

Tanto mejor.   All the better!

¡Con razón!   No wonder!

¿Está bueno?   Is it good?

¡Está bueno!   That's good!

HOT TIPS!

- Caution! Rudeness will ruin communication!
- These one-liners are great at *fiestas*! Here, for example, is a bit of one-liner dialogue.
  Maria: *¿Listo?* (Ready?)
  Carlos: *Creo que sí. ¿Y Tomás?* (I think so. And Thomas?)
  Maria: *¡Ahí viene!* (Here he comes!)
  Carlos: *¿Y Carolina?* (And Carolina?)
  Maria: *¡Ya se fue!* (She's left!)
  Carlos: *¡Está bueno!* (That's good!)

Más One-liners

No entiendo or *No comprendo.*
   I don't understand.
A la vez.   At the same time.
Muchas veces.   Lots of times.
Una vez.   One time.

No sé.   I don't know.

Todavía no.   Not yet.
Ahora no.   Not now.
En punto.   On time.

Al revés.   Backwards.
Boca abajo.   Upside down.

These four expressions are often used instead of *adiós.*

¡Vaya con Dios!   Go with God!
¡Dios le bendiga!   God bless you!
¡Buen Viaje!   Have a nice trip!
Me saluda a...   Give my regards to...

Use these expressions, but with *emoción* (emotion)!

¡Felicitaciones!   Congratulations!
¡Feliz Navidad!   Merry Christmas!
¡Feliz cumpleaños!   Happy Birthday!

¡Socorro!   Help!
¡Caramba!   Wow!
¡Dios mío!   For heaven's sake!

¡Mentiras!   Lies!
¡Basta!   Enough!
¡Vaya!   Go on!
¡Vámonos!   Let's go!

Es muy...
It's very...

cierto   certain
correcto   correct
fantástico   fantastic
importante   important
interesante   interesting
necesario   necessary
obvio   obvious
terrible   terrible

¡Qué...

barbaridad!   How awful!
bueno!   How great!
chiste!   What a joke!
disfrute!   Have a good time!
extraño!   How strange!
lástima!   What a shame!
le vaya bien!   Take care!
se alivie!   Get well!
suerte!   What luck!
tiene!   So what!
triste!   How sad!
va!   Pshaw, go on!

To learn even more one-liners, *listen carefully* and *ask* Spanish speakers what words and phrases mean! Repeat and practice alone until you *feel* prepared. Instead of writing these phrases, just memorize the sounds!

"Close Encounters"

If you've been paying attention, this will *not* be difficult. All you do is try to figure out what would be the best "natural" response. Write it only if you want to. Go ahead and use any of the words and phrases introduced so far.

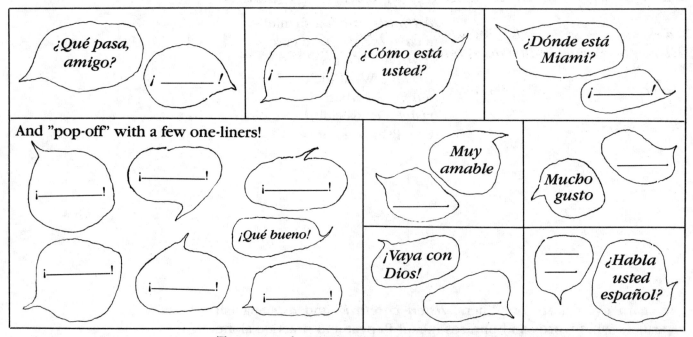

Try more than one response. Check any previous page for possible responses. And, just as you would do in an actual situation—be creative!

Fantastic *Frases*

For the bravest of babblers, here are some "advanced plays" that truly make folks sound like they know what they're talking about.

Por eso... Therefore...	*A propósito...* By the way...
O sea... In other words...	*Al principio...* At first...
Además... Besides...	*Por lo menos...* At least...
Por fin... At last...	*Según...* According to...
Por ejemplo... For example...	*En general...* In general...
Sobre todo... Above all...	*Paso a paso...* Step by step...
Sin embargo... However...	*Poco a poco...* Little by little...

Here's an example of how it's done.

¿Mi carro? **En general,** *mi carro es excelente.* My car? In general, my car is good.

Por ejemplo, *el color es perfecto.*   For example, the color is perfect.

Además, *es muy grande.*   Besides, it's very big.

Sin embargo, *el motor no es bueno.*   However, the engine isn't any good.

¿Mi carro? No sé.   My car? I don't know.

Now, you try it!

I Have a *Pregunta* (Question)

Tengo una [handwritten annotation]

Suggestions for Success

Try to apply the following suggestions when making questions and giving answers in Spanish.

- **Focus on the first word!** There are only a few "question words," so learn them. The next step is to listen for main words in the question that you can recognize or "guess at." Concentrate on the "topic" of conversation.

- **Answer as briefly as possible!** Take your time. And if you want, repeat the question you've been asked. At first, only respond with key words and short phrases.

- **Relax and remember your English!** Whether you're asking or answering, try using each word just as you would in English. Again, it's OK to mix both languages if you should forget!

The Primary *Preguntas* in *Español*

Make *muy* sure you can both understand and say the lifesaving *pregunta* words that follow:

¿*Cuál?*   What/Which?
¿*Cómo?*   How?
¿*Qué?*   What?
¿*Dónde?*   Where?
¿*Cuánto?*   How much?
¿*Cuántos?*   How many?
¿*Cuándo?*   When?
¿*Quién?*   Who?

HOT TIPS!

- All the *pregunta* words need accent marks. A few change meaning when you drop the accent: *como* (I eat) and *que* (that).
- Always put a "¿" at the beginning of a question, as well as the "?" at the end. **¿De acuerdo?**

¿*Cuál*…? (What or which…?)

Let's begin with the **cuál** questions; which can sometimes be answered with one or two words. Here are the most common questions needed to get basic information:

¿**Cuál** *es su nombre?*   What is your name?   *Mi nombre es Juan.*
¿**Cuál** *es su dirección?*   What's your address?   *Mi dirección es 363 Main St.*
¿**Cuál** *es su número de teléfono?*   What's your phone number? *Mi número es 555-1234.*
¿**Cuál** *es su lugar de nacimiento?*   What's your place of birth?   *Mi lugar de nacimiento es Havana.*

¿**Cuál** *es su libro?*   Which (one) is your book?
¿**Cuál** *es su lápiz?*   Which (one) is your pencil?
¿**Cuál** *es su cuaderno?*   Which (one) is your notebook?

¿**Cuál** *es su* _____?

Make your own.

- ¿*Cuál?* all by itself means, "Which one?" ¿*Cuáles?* means "Which ones" and is the word for "which" when there are *more than one*.

Anillo - ring
dorado, golden
Y mi anillo de oro
¿ un anillo dorado?

Nombre News (Juan, José, López, Pérez)

Keep in mind the following when you ask for a person's name.

- *¿Cómo se llama?* is another way to ask "What's your name?"
- *Primer nombre* is "first name."
- *Apellido* is "last name."

Juan   José
Primer nombre
(Not all Hispanic people have
two first names!)

López
Apellido paternal
(Dad's)

Pérez
Apellido maternal
(Mom's)

NOTES
- In the United States, this guy is just *Juan López.*
- When a woman marries, she keeps her dad's last name, followed by her husband's.
- There's no "middle name" as we know it.

¿Cómo?

All alone, *¿Cómo?* means *"What?"* or "How's that?" Use it like "How?" The classic *¿Cómo se llama?* literally means. "How are you called?" Now, can you tackle these other *cómo* concepts?

- *¿Cómo se dice?*   How do you say it?
- *¿Cómo se escribe?*   How do you write it?
- *¿Cómo está?*   How are you?

¿Qué?

¿Qué? always means "What?" as in *¿Qué pasa?* (What's happening?) Here are more *qué* classics:

Point to something and ask:
- *¿Qué es esto?*   What's this?

- *¿Qué es eso?*   What's that?
- *¿Qué son?*   What are they?
- *¿Qué significa?*   What does it mean?
- *¿Qué hora es?*   What time is it?

HOT TIPS!

- **Slow down,** relax! Ask your questions and give your answers *palabra por palabra* (word by word), *letra por letra* (letter by letter), or *número por número* (number by number).
- *Su* means "his," "her," or "its" in addition to "your." SO POINT!
- *¿Qué?* can also be used to mean, "What"?: *¿Qué pasa?* What is happening?

(handwritten notes at top: 700 pent   100 EU / 40   DM   1.00 EU / 12 / 10,000. lire   1,00 EU / 115. =)

¿Dónde?

¿Dónde? is for direction; it is the "Where?" word. Whether you're looking for a person, place, or thing, just fill in the blank:

¿Dónde está   (Where's) _____?
"Look for" these phrases also:

¿Dónde vive?   Where do you live?

¿Dónde trabaja?   Where do you work?

¿Adónde va?   Where are you going?

¿De dónde es?   Where are you from?

¿Cuánto?

¿Cuánto(a)? (How much?) is the shopping word. *¿Cuántos(as)?* means "How many?" These words need the *El* (masculine) and *La* (feminine) Business. You can always "count" on these phrases:

¿Cuántos años tiene?   How old are you?

¿Cuánto tiempo?   How much time?

¿Cuánto cuesta?   How much does it cost?

(handwritten: no se — I don't know)

¿Quién?

¿Quién es? means "Who is it?"
¿A quién?...   To whom...?
¿Quiénes son?   Who are they?
¿Para quién?...   For whom...?
¿De quién?...   From whom...?   *carta*

NOTE
Words change
a bit when you want to
refer to *past* action. Don't
be concerned! For now,
use these as you would
one-liners:
¿Cuándo nació?   When
were you born?
Fue ayer. It was yesterday.
¿Qué pasó?   What
happened?

¿Cuándo?

We'll be reading the clock and calendar soon, so let's warm up with some *¿Cuándo?* quickies.

¿Cuándo...	*empieza?*	does it begin?
When...	*termina?*	does it end?
	llega?	does it arrive?
	sale?	does it leave?
	nació usted?	were you born?

Long responses to these questions sound strange—so avoid using complex sentences. Keep those answers short!

¿Cuándo llega usted? —

Ayer.	Yesterday.
Ahora.	Today.
Mañana.	Tomorrow.

If you feel that you've had enough for now, take a break! Walk around, name things, or try out new words you've already learned. I'll be here when you get back!

Who's Who?

To really get going, you've got to know these important words, which can designate the **"who"** of a *quién(es)* question.

Use these words as you do their English equivalents and don't forget to point.

Yo   I

Usted   You

Ella   She

Él   He

Ellos   They

Ustedes   You guys

Nosotros   We

Note:
Ellas = "They," feminine;
Nosotras = "We," feminine.

HOT TIPS!

- The preceding *quién* words (subject pronouns) work wonderfully as one-word responses. Notice how they also "start you off" when expressing a complete message: *¿Quién es inteligente?—Ella es inteligente.* (Who is intelligent?—She is intelligent.)
- *Él, ella, ellos,* and *ellas* can refer to things as well as as people: *Los libros, ¿dónde están ellos?* (The books, where are they?)
- "Grab onto" the first word in all questions, because they will make answering so much easier!

Posesión (Possession)

mi *amigo*
my friend

su *amigo*
their, your, his, or her friend

nuestro *amigo*
our friend

Just add "s" to both words (possessive adjective and noun) when talking about more than one.

- *mis amigos*
- *sus amigos*
- *nuestros amigos*

¿De quién es? (Whose is it?)

If someone (or something) "belongs to" someone else use **de** (of/from) to tell who the person is:

It's Maria's friend.

*Es el amigo **de** María.*

The *Posesión* Principles

- Don't forget the *El* and *La* Business:
  nuestra amiga   our friend

- Don't get possessive words (adjectives) mixed up with *quién* words (pronouns):
  Yo *tengo* ***mi*** *carro.*   I have **my** car.

- Try these possessive words once in a while:
  Es…   *mío.*   mine.
  It's   *suyo.*   yours, his, hers, *or* theirs.

- When you get stuck, escape with ***de!***
  ¿Es él un amigo ***de…usted?***   yours?
                                 él?   his?
                                 ella?   hers?
  Is he a friend **of**   ***ellos?***   theirs (masculine)?
                                 ellas?   theirs (feminine)?
                               ustedes?   yours?

- Perhaps you haven't noticed, but sometimes *en español,* it's OK to drop the *quién* word! It's already understood who's involved.
  (Yo) ***Estoy*** *bien.*   I'm fine.

The Reversal Rule

In speaking Spanish, it is sometimes necessary to *think backwards!* For example, if you'd like to *describe* something, just *reverse* the order of the describing word and that of what's being described:

A lot of **good tacos.**
*Muchos **tacos buenos.***

HOT TIPS!

- When you talk, try to recall the Once-and-for-All Rule and the *El* and *La* Business (feminine and masculine gender). But *don't let this slow you down.* Forgetting sometimes won't hurt anything!

- You'll probably encounter *muchos ejemplos más* (many more examples), but *fear not*—you'll catch on!

…The same goes for *posesión,* Spanish first tells what belongs, then to whom it belongs:

John's house.
*La **casa** de **Juan.***

…As well as for giving addresses:
642 Broadway Avenue
Avenida Broadway 642

…In addition to some "action" words, which are sometimes reversed:
I like coffee.
Me gusta el café or *El café me gusta.*

…And many one-liners:
Not now!
¡Ahora no!

¡Entrevista!
(Interview!)

If you're truly serious about learning *español,* the *Entrevista* is for you. Here's how it works. Simply "prepare" three common questions and then write one in each top box to the right of the words *Los nombres* (names). See chart below. Next, go some place nearby where you can easily "interview" Spanish speakers. List their names under **Los Nombres.** (To get their names, use Question 1.) *Fill in their responses* in the boxes to the right under each question.

> **NOTE**
> Use a clipboard!

(Los nombres) Names	¿Cuál es su nombre? (What's your name?)	¿Cómo está usted? (How are you?)	¿De dónde es usted? (Where are you from?)
José López	José	bien	Puerto Rico
María Sánchez			
Luis Pérez			

INFORMACIÓN IMPORTANTE

- The more Spanish you learn, the more "complex" your questions will become. No need to "force it" now.
- Spend time chatting with folks you interview. It's fun!
- Start slowly. Practice first with people you are familiar with.
- A three-question interview like this takes *less than 2 minutes* per person. "Too busy" is *no excuse!*
- If you should have trouble understanding, just have them "write-in" their own responses!
- Your approach should be friendly. Stop strangers with *"Disculpe."* ("Excuse me.") *"Estoy en un programa de español."* ("I'm in a Spanish program.") *"Quiero hacerle tres preguntas."* ("I want to ask you three questions.") *"Muchas gracias."* ("Thanks a lot.") Trust me. They'll *love* to help!

The *Super-preguntas*

¿Cuál? _____	
¿Cómo? _____	
¿Qué? _____	
¿Dónde? _____	
¿Cuántos? _____	
¿Cuánto? _____	
¿Quién? _____	
¿Cuándo? _____	

Without checking, can you give the meanings of these basic question words?

The following are *más* than just survival questions—they're *super!*

¿Le gusta?   Do you* like it?

¿Entiende?   Do you* understand?

¿Quisiera?   Would you (he, she) like some?

¿Hay?   Is there…*or* Are there any?

¿Por qué?   Why? *(Porque,* without the accent, is "Because")

¿Quiere?   Do you* want it?

¿Tiene?   Do you* have some?

¿Puede?   Can you (he, she) do it?

*Also: Does he *or* Does she .

HOT TIPS!

- For the moment, use the *super-preguntas* just like a one-liner!
- The *super-preguntas* are even *more powerful* when other words are added. Take a chance and add words you already know:

  ¿Le gusta…   Do you like…(the wine, beer, etc.)?

  ¿Entiende usted… Do you understand… (English, the problem, etc.)?

  ¿Quisiera usted… Would you like… (soda, coffee, etc.)?

  ¿Hay…   Are there a lot of…(people, books, etc.)?

  ¿Por qué…   Why don't you…(like it, etc.)?

  ¿Quiere usted…   Do you want…(more sauce, etc.)?

  ¿Tiene usted…   Do you have a…(car, good idea, etc.)?

- Once you "get" that first word, next try focusing on exactly what it is they are asking you!

4

CHAPTER *CUATRO*
Mucho más
(Much More)

Do You Know Your ABC's? (*El alfabeto*)

¿Cómo se dice?

Once you get rolling, you'll find yourself asking people everywhere how to say things *en español.* At work, in public, or on the phone— learning words will simply be part of your everyday routine. Remember the following *preguntas?* Well, go ahead and use them to "pry."

¿Qué es esto?   What's this?
¿Cómo se dice?   How do you say it?
¿Qué significa?   What does it mean?

They're *importantes,* yet sometimes you'll have to ask folks to "write it for you." Here's a line that may help:

¿Cómo se escribe?   How do you write it?

Simply hand them a pen and ask for it *"Letra por letra, por favor."* ("Letter by letter, please.")

El alfabeto

First, the *easy* part:

1 You already know the Big Five—*a, e, i, o, u*—their names are just as they sound!

2 Well, these letters are "close" to English:

b (beh "larga" or "grande")   *n* (eh'-neh)
v (beh "corta" or "chica")   *p* (peh)
c (seh)   *q* (coo)
d (deh)   *r* (eh'-reh)
f (eh'-feh)   *s* (eh'-seh)
k (kah)   *t* (teh)
b (ah'cheh)   *w* (beh doh'-bleh)
l (eh'-leh)   *x* (eh'-kees)
m (eh'-meh)

3 And here we have the four Spanish letters most gringos have problems with:

g (heh) *j* (ho'-tah) *y* (ee-gree-eh'-gah) *z* (seh'-tah)

4 The alfabeto also has **four more "letters"** than ours. Three of them are spelled with two letters together. And one has a ˜ on top!:

cb (cheh) *ll* (eh'-yeh) *rr* (eh'-rreh) *ñ* (en'-yeh)

5 *Muy bien.* Are you ready to read the *alfabeto* in order? (Go somewhere "private" and *sing* it!)

a, b, c, cb, d, e, f, g, b, i, j, k, l, ll,
m, n, ñ, o, p, q, r, rr, s, t, u, v, w, x, y, z.

HOT TIPS!

- Spell *everything aloud* in Spanish from now on!
- But first, learn to spell your *nombre* and other *información de emergencia* (emergency information) just in case!
- Practice spelling over the *teléfono!*
- Use your *Diccionario* often! And practice looking up words ALOUD!
- Try teaching *inglés* words to a Spanish-speaking person. You'll be forced to spell!
- As you learned from the Secrets to Soundmaking, "close" is good enough!

Take a *Número* (Number)

0   1   2   3   4   5   6 *sez*   7   8   9

> If you don't know these numbers, go back to *"Viva el vocabulario!"*

Sure, *los números* are easy. But do you realize how valuable they really are? In most cases, just by stating one number at a time, you can save yourself *muchos problemas!*

¿Cuál es su...
What is your...

> Go ahead, answer the following "personal information," *número por número:*

número de teléfono   (phone number)? ___ *siete tres siete ocho zero cinco zero*

dos zero siete, tres zero cinco cinco cinco dos
número de seguro social   (social security number)? ___

número de licencia de chofer   (driver's license number)? ___

domicilio or dirección   (address)? *nuevo*
código postal   (zip code)? *zero quatro tres cinco siete*
código de área   (area code)? *dos zero siete*
número de póliza   (policy number)? ___
número de placa   (license plate number)? *ocho zero tres ocho*
número de tarjeta de crédito   (credit card number)? ___

You get the idea. Daily, practice saying aloud everything from your pocket change to the TV channels. *Remember* that the trick is to keep it fun!

Take Some More Numbers

Let's begin by breaking down *los números* just as we did the Spanish *alfabeto*—it helps the memory. Use your own word-association system, and stay motivated by thinking of new and exciting ways you can use to practice *every day!*

1 First, some *weird* numbers:
  10 *diez*
  11 *once*
  20 *veinte* vénte

Practice these three until you can say them quickly and without *problemas!*

2 Next, the *easiest* ones:
  12 *doce* (Hear the *"dos"?*)
  13 *trece* (Hear the "tres"?)

3 Now, try to *picture these:*
  14 *ca**tor**ce* (The number looks kind of "con**tor**ted")
  15 *quince* (Pronounced "Kings say")

4 And how about some *math?*
  (10) *diez y seis* (6) = 16
      diez y siete = 17
      diez y ocho = 18
      diez y nueve = 19

5 These multiples of *10* all end in—*nta!*:
  Listen for the:
  30 ***trei**nta*   *(**tres**)*
  40 ***cua**renta*   *(**cua**tro)*
  50 ***cincu**enta*   *(**cinc**o)*
  60 ***ses**enta*   *(**seis**)*
  70 ***set**enta*   *(**siete**)*
  80 ***och**enta*   *(**och**o)*
  90 ***nov**enta*   *(**nueve**)*

6 The numbers between are *all math problems!*:
  (20) *veinte y uno* (1) = (21) *veintiuno*
  ____ *veinte y dos* ___ = (22) *veintidos*
  ____ *veinte y tres* ___ = (23) *veintitres*
  ____ _____ ___ = ____

NOTE

In Spanish, check out the difference in the numerical form of the ordinals:
1st = 1ª or 1º
2nd = 2ª or 2º
3rd = 3ª or 3º
...and so on.

NOTE

Three more "toughies":
500 = *quinientos*
700 = *setecientos*
900 = *novecientos*
And guess what these are:
millón?   *billón?*

NOTE

Primero and *tercero* lose their final letter when placed in front of masculine singular words:
Mi primer carro.   My first car.
Está en el tercer grado.   He is in third grade.

7   100 is *cien.* (like, "**cen**tury")
101 is *ciento* (+) *uno.*
201 is *dos cientos* (+) *uno.*

500 quinientos
600 —
700 — setecientos

8   1000 is *mil.* (like, "**mill**ennium")
2000 is *dos mil,* etc.

9   **Order Up!**
1**st** *primera, – o*
2**nd** *segunda, – o*
3**rd** *tercera, – o*
4**th** *cuarta, – o*
5**th** *quinta, – o*
6**th** *sexta, – o*
7**th** *séptima, – o*
8**th** *octava, – o*
9**th** *novena, – o*
10**th** *decima, – o*

Instant Time Telling

Learning to tell someone what time it is in Spanish will take *no time* at all! Although there are other optional ways to do it, this is clearly the easiest and fastest way to go:

¿Qué hora es?
What time is it?

Listen for *"hora"* which means "the hour."

¿Qué horas son? means the same thing.

NOTE

The *only change* is "half past." Then you say **y media** or **y treinta:** 6:30 = *seis y media.*

To say, **"It's**—2:00 or more—use **Son las**...*dos, tres,* etc. (You don't say "o'clock.")

If it's 1:00–1:59 then use **Es la**...instead!

Try these: 7:45, 9:00, 1:30

...To answer, just look at your **reloj** (a watch or clock!) and give the **hora** followed by the **minutos.**

6:15
seis, quince

OTHER "TIMELY TIDBITS"

...in the **morning**   *de la mañana*
...in the **afternoon**   *de la tarde*
...in the **evening**   *de la noche*
Noon   *mediodía*
Midnight   *medianoche*

If you want to say "**At** (a certain time)," say **A las**...
Tiempo means "time, in general"
En punto means "on the dot"
Segundos are "seconds."

HOT TIPS!

- To tell time...notice you only need to know 1–59.
- Have others teach you some other ways to tell time!

International Date Line

Still another practical use of *los números* is the yearly calendar. Let's begin with the most common words and phrases having to do with **el calendario** (the calendar):

el día   the day
el mes   the month
la semana   the week
el año   the year

¡El calendario!

los días de la semana

el lunes	Monday
el martes	Tuesday
el miércoles	Wednesday
el jueves	Thursday
el viernes	Friday
el sábado	Saturday
el domingo	Sunday

los meses del año

1	enero	5	mayo
2	febrero	6	junio
3	marzo	7	julio
4	abril	8	agosto

9	septiembre
10	octubre
11	noviembre
12	diciembre

¿Cuál es la fecha?   What's the date?

The year is always read as one large number:

1990 =   *mil   novecientos   noventa*
                1000   900   90

And whenever you give the date, apply the "Reversal Rule"!

June 3rd
el tres de junio

CHOOSE 'n USE!

Los días

Hay una fiesta...   There's a party...(on Saturday, on Friday, etc.)

¿Trabaja usted...?   Do you work...(on Monday, etc.)

El programa empieza...   The program begins...(on Thursday, etc.)

Los meses

Ayer fue el ____ de ____   Yesterday was the (20th, etc.) of...- (August, etc.)

Mi cumpleaños es en...   My birthday is in...(February, etc.)

¿Tiene usted las vacaciones en...?   Do you have vacation in...? (October, etc.)

Calendar Express!

Besides the basic calendar words it's nice to have other key words and expressions that will help get any date-line message across. As always, practice these *aloud* first, before you actually "go for it"!

The "*¿Qué día*" questions:

- *¿Qué día es hoy?*   **What day** is today?
- *¿Qué día es mañana?*   **What day** is tomorrow?
- *¿Qué día fue ayer?*   **What day** was yesterday?
- *¿Qué día fue anteayer?*   **What day** was the day before yesterday?
- *¿Qué día es pasado mañana?*   **What day** is the day after tomorrow?

¡*Las estaciones!* (The Seasons!)

la primavera   spring

el otoño   fall

el verano   summer

el invierno   winter

*¿Cuál es **su** estación favorita?* _____. (Which is **your** favorite season?)

¡Más palabras importantes en el calendario!

HOT TIP!

Hay ("there is" or "there are")
is a **muy** useful calendar word! **Hay** una fiesta mañana!"

el próximo   the next one
el pasado   the past one
actual   current
ahora   now; nowadays

el aniversario   anniversary
la cita   appointment
diario   daily
la fiesta   party
el fin de semana   week-end
el horario   schedule
la junta   meeting
las vacaciones   vacation

How's the Weather? (*¿Qué tiempo hace?*)

Making conversation with "weather chit-chat" is a *must* in any language and *¿Qué tiempo hace?* is a question that's *excelente* as an ice-breaker. Then, you're bound to need these:

Hace...
It's

frío	cold
calor	hot
viento	windy
sol	sunny
buen tiempo	nice weather

Está...

It's

despejado	clear
nublado	cloudy
nevando	snowing
lloviendo	raining
lloviznando	drizzling

Más Weather Words:

el agua	water	*el huracán*	hurricane
el aire	air	*la luna*	moon
el cielo	sky	*la marea*	tide
las estrellas	stars	*los relámpagos*	lightning
el fuego	fire	*el terremoto*	earthquake
los grados	degrees	*la tormenta*	storm
el hielo	ice	*el trueno*	thunder
el humo	smoke, smog	*el tornado*	tornado

HOT TIPS!

- Here's the *easy way!*

  Hay...
  There is
  or
  There are

neblina	fog
nubes	clouds
lluvia	rain
nieva	snow
humo	smog

- If the *weather* is *not* moderate, use:

  ¡Hace mucho calor!
  It's very hot!
  ¡Hace mucho frío!
  It's very cold!
  nieva mucho
  It **snows** a lot
  llueve mucho
  It **rains** a lot

- *El clima* means "the climate."

5

CHAPTER *CINCO*
Las personas
(People)

Es versus Está

> ## NOTE
>
> Look closely! (Read this section twice!)
> *Yo estoy aquí y estoy contento.*
> I am here and I am happy.
> *Ustedes están aquí y están contentos.*
> They are here and they're happy.
> *Nosotros estamos aquí y estamos contentos.*
> We are here and we're happy.
> (See? *Estar* is used to indicate current "condition" or "location" only.)
> *Yo soy Italiano.*
> I am Italian.
> *Ustedes son altos.*
> You guys are tall.
> *Nosotros somos de Chile.*
> We're from Chile.
> (*Ser* is used to indicate "who" or "what" is.)

Are you totally confused about the uses of **es** *and* **está?**

I say *es!*

I say *está!*

STOP THE FIGHT!

They're both right.

In Spanish, to say **is** or **you are**, it's **está** when referring to:

- **Location**   *¿Dónde* **está** *Carlos? —Él está allá!*
- **Condition**   *¿Cómo* **está** *Lupe? —Ella está muy bien.*

To indicate **"who"** or **"what" is,** use *es:*

Usted **es** *inteligente— Si, pero, usted* **es** *mas inteligente.*
María **es** *mexicana— No, ella* **es** *cubana.*

Notice the difference!

- ***Está***
  Él **está** *bien.*   He **is** fine.
  La silla no **está** *en la sala.*   The chair **is** not in the living room.
  Ella **está** *trabajando.*   She **is** working.
- ***Es***
  El programa **es** *importante.*   The program **is** important.
  María **es** *profesora.*   Maria **is** a professor.
  *¿***Es** *usted puertorriqueña?*   **Are** you Puerto Rican?

That's all you get for now! All this stuff is further explained in Chapter *Siete*.

Get it Together—Part I

It's time to begin linking your *palabras* together! Strings of words bound by logic create meaningful messages. And remembering that pronunciation and grammar have little effect on communication allows us to "babble away" more freely. Another helpful trick to recall is that words are joined in much the same order in Spanish as they are in *inglés!*

When we speak *single words* and *one-liners* are the easiest ways to communicate our ideas:

> *¡Sí!*   Yes!
> *Él es.*   He is.

And adding words "to clarify" is *not* difficult:

> *¡Sí!, él es mi amigo.*   He is my friend.

Only, remember to use the "little linkers" —*y* (and), *o* (or), ***pero*** (but):

> *Él es mi amigo y ella es mi amiga,...*
> *...¡**pero** ella es más inteligente!*   ...**but** she is more intelligent!

Do you remember any of this stuff?
El libro de José   Jose's book
es azul y rojo,   is blue and red,
pero está en su casa.   but it's at his house.
¿Cómo se llama?   What's your name?
¿Y dónde vive?   And where do you live?
En diciembre, hay nubes y hace mucho frío, y llueve mucho.
In December, it's cloudy and very cold, and it rains a lot.

Moreover, don't worry about "getting stuck." Just plug in an English word. (Although the last option may elicit a wince or a laugh from your listener.)

> *Él es mi amigo y ella es mi amiga, pero ella es más inteligente y más **rich!***

HOT TIPS!

- First, try *es* or *está*. Then, if your listener seems confused, smile and try it another way!
- In linking your Spanish words, recall and use these three concepts:
  1. The Reversal Rule
  2. The Once-and-for-all Rule
  3. The *El* and *La* Business
- Your Spanish pronunciation will improve the more you speak.

HOT TIPS!

- Here's what the *tú* form looks like:
  ¿Cómo estás tú?
  How are **you?**
  Es para ti.   It's for
  you.
  Yo te quiero mucho.
  I love **you** a lot.
  *Tu casa es
  bonita.*   **Your**
  house is beautiful.
  ¿Es la tuya?   Is it
  yours?

- **If you ever come
  across Ud. or Uds.**
  in your Spanish read-
  ing, don't fret!
  They're abbreviations
  for *Usted* and
  Ustedes.

Un Comentario
about *the "tu" form*

Some readers might be wondering why I've only mentioned the "formal" *usted* form, and not the *tú* or so-called informal form of *es* and *está*. Think about it. *Why bother?* It just becomes another thing GRINGOS have to worry about. Spanish-speaking people use the intimate *tú* when speaking to their friends. But that's because they can understand each other! And they're bound by cultural ties. My point here is simple. By following these shortcuts, tips and Secrets to Success, *you too* will be able to make friends and establish "informal" relationships with Spanish-speaking people. Soon your new pals will be teaching you the *tú* form, along with lots of other "inside info." Besides, the *usted* form is easier to remember and use. You'll find it's perfectly acceptable when speaking with *anyone!*

"How Ya Doin'?"

We've talked already briefly about the question: *¿Cómo está usted?* (How are you?) We know that the answer, *Muy bien* (Very well), is the old stand-by! Now let's check out the many other responses that tell folks **how you feel.**

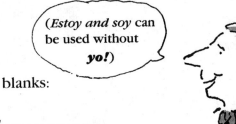

(*Estoy and soy* can be used without **yo!**)

If you want, try filling in the blanks:

> *Yo estoy* _____ .
> *Yo soy* _____ .
> (**I** am…)

fantástico(a)	fantastic	*sorprendido(a)*	surprised
bien	well	*cansado(a)*	tired
regular	OK	*orgulloso(a)*	proud
así-así	not bad	*débil*	weak
mal	not well	*fuerte*	strong
enfermo(a)	sick	*dormido(a)*	sleepy
feliz	happy	*aburrido(a)*	bored
triste	sad	*ansioso(a)*	anxious
ocupado(a)	busy	*enojado(a)*	angry
preocupado(a)	worried		
nervioso(a)	nervous		

CHOOSE 'N USE!
- Estoy un poco…   I'm a little…(tired, sleepy, etc.).
- ¿Está usted muy…? Are you very…(bored, anxious, etc.)?
- Carol está demasiado…y…   Carol is too…(sad, etc.) and…(worried).
- ¿Está…usted?   Are you…(surprised, etc.)?
- Es…él?   Is he a…(happy, sad, etc.) person?

NOTE
Es and *está* change what you're trying to say about a person's condition:
El ***está*** *nervioso.*   He is nervous.
El ***es*** *nervioso.*   He's a nervous person.

¡Que cuerpo!
(What a Body!)

It's time to learn the Spanish names for different parts of the human body. After all, people are made *de carne y hueso* (of flesh and bone):

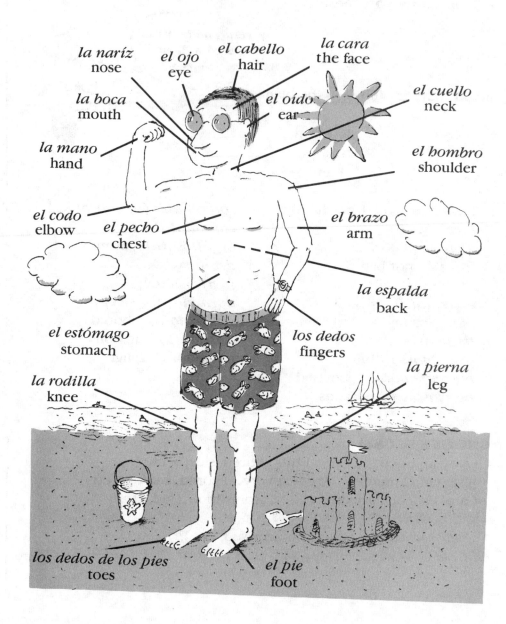

la naríz — nose
el ojo — eye
el cabello — hair
la cara — the face
la boca — mouth
el oído — ear
el cuello — neck
la mano — hand
el hombro — shoulder
el codo — elbow
el pecho — chest
el brazo — arm
la espalda — back
el estómago — stomach
los dedos — fingers
la rodilla — knee
la pierna — leg
los dedos de los pies — toes
el pie — foot

¡Ayyy! (Ouch!)

Here are some Spanish words and phrases to help you express what may go wrong with the body.

el accidente   accident
la ambulancia   ambulance
la contusión   bruise
la cortada   cut
la Cruz Roja   Red Cross
el dolor   pain
la emergencia   emergency
la fiebre   fever
la herida   wound
el hueso quebrado   broken
   bone
los primeros auxilios   first aid
la sangre   blood

Dolor de...

espalda   back ache
muela   tooth ache
cabeza   head ache
garganta   sore throat
estómago   stomach ache

Me duele.   It hurts.
Me siento mejor.   I feel better.
Estoy malo(a).   I'm ill.
Estoy débil.   I'm weak.
Tengo resfriado.   I have a cold.

Tengo resfriado en el pecho.   I have a cold in my chest.
Tengo la fiebre en la cabeza.   I have a fever.
Me duele el estómago.   My stomach hurts.
¿Hay dolor en el cuello?   Is there a pain in the neck?
¿Hay cortadas en los brazos?   Are there cuts on the arms?
¿Hay los huesos quebrados en las piernas?   Are there broken bones in the legs?
¡Llame al doctor!   Call the doctor!

Family Ties

La gente and *las personas* both mean "the people."

Without a doubt, one of your initial encounters in Spanish will eventually lead to speaking about family members. But before we take a look at *la familia*, let's first make an effort to master these *muy importante* "people" *palabras:*

el hombre   man
la mujer   woman
el niño   small boy
la niña   small girl
el muchacho   young boy
la muchacha   young girl
el bebé   baby

el señor or *Sr.*   a man or Mr.
la señora or *Sra.*   a lady or Mrs.
la señorita or *Srta.*   a young unmarried woman
la persona   person

el amigo   friend
el enemigo   enemy

los amantes   lovers
el novio   boyfriend or groom
la novia   girlfriend or bride
los novios   sweethearts or bride and groom

los parientes   relatives
los hijos   sons and daughters
los hermanos   brothers or brother and sister
los papás or *padres*   parents
los abuelos   grandparents

HOT TIPS!

- Make the necessary changes for feminine and masculine, according to the *El* and *La* Business.
- To make more sentences, go ahead and insert words from both of the following categories.
  ¿Quién? words:
  yo, usted, ella, él, ellos nosotros, ustedes.
  ¡Posesión! words:
  mi, mis, su, sus, nuestro, nuestros.

Ella es **mi** amiga.

Más "Persona" Palabras!
alguien   someone
nadie   no one
cualquier persona   anyone
todo el mundo   everybody
poca gente   a few people
mucha gente   a lot of people
los compañeros   buddies

CHOOSE 'N USE!

- *Lupe es...*   Lupe is...(my small boy, my friend, etc.).
- *...está aquí.*   The...(man, baby, etc.) is here.
- *¿Quién es...?*   Who is the...(person, enemy, etc.)?
- *¿Son sus...?*   Are they your...(relatives, grandparents, etc.)?
- *Me gustan sus...*   I like your...(parents, brothers, etc.).
- *¿Dónde están...?*   Where are the...(lovers, sweethearts, etc.)?

NOTE
Los padrinos are "godparents"—in most Spanish-speaking countries, the in-laws and godparents are considered important family members! *Los compadres* is the name parents and godparents of a child share.

Los miembros de la familia
(The Family Members)

Touch these pictures with your finger. Read aloud, and check for meanings!

Él He   **Ella** She
Su his, her, your, or their

Él es su esposo	*Ella es su esposa*
Él es su padre	*Ella es su madre*
Él es su hermano	*Ella es su hermana*
Él es su hijo	*Ella es su hija*
Él es su abuelo	*Ella es su abuela*

el padre	father	*el yerno*	son-in-law
la madre	mother	*la nuera*	daughter-in-law
el abuelo	grandfather	*el cuñado*	brother-in-law
la abuela	grandmother	*la cuñada*	sister-in-law
el tío	uncle	*la hermana*	sister
la tía	aunt	*el hermano*	brother
el esposo or *el marido*	husband	*el hijo*	son
la esposa	wife	*la hija*	daughter
el suegro	father-in-law	*los nietos*	grandchildren
la suegra	mother-in-law	*los primos*	cousins

Familia fine points:

- The family unit is a vital part of Hispanic culture. Be sensitive.
- Other "terms of endearment" may be used besides the preceding words to name family members. Learn by asking or look them up in the dictionary if you need to.
- Notice how the informal *tú* is used for you instead of *usted* when family and friends talk to each other.
- Use *es! Por ejemplo* (For example):

Es... He's or She's
mayor   older *que than*
menor   younger
un(a) gemelo(a)   a twin
casado(a)   married
soltero(a)   single

Él (Ella) *es*...

joven   young
viejo(a)   old
anciano(a)   very old

HOT TIP!

For affection, *-ita* and *-ito* can be added:
abuelita
hermanito
bebito

divorciado
— divorced

los hijos tienen la misma edad
same age

¡Mucho trabajo!
(A Lot of Work!)

Most folks don't spend all of their time "hanging around" the relatives at home. They go to work. Let's expand our "people-talk" to include the words needed to chat about work.

Los trabajadores (The workers)

el abogado	lawyer	*el enfermero*	nurse
el arquitecto	architect	*el estudiante*	student
el asistente	assistant	*el gerente*	office manager
el bombero	fireman	*el ingeniero*	engineer
el cajero	cashier	*el jardinero*	gardener
el camarero or *mesero*	waiter	*el jefe*	boss
el camionero	truck driver	*el maestro*	teacher
el campesino	farmer	*el mecánico*	mechanic
el carpintero	carpenter	*el músico*	musician
el cliente	client	*el pintor*	painter
el cocinero	chef	*el plomero*	plumber
el criado	servant	*el policía*	policeman
el dentista	dentist	*el secretario*	secretary
el dependiente	clerk	*el soldado*	soldier
el doctor	doctor	*el trabajador de*	
el dueño	owner	*fábrica*	factory worker
el empleado	employee	*el vendedor*	salesman

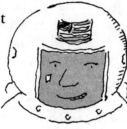

Some rather unique *profesiones:*

el payaso clown
el astronauta astronaut
la actríz actress

el atleta athlete
el ladrón thief
el escritor writer

HOT TIPS!

- *¿Qué hace?* means "What do you do?" (also, What does *he* or *she* do?)
- Make sentences! Just put **Es** in front! (**Es** = he's, she's, you're)
- *Sí,* these words **do** require the *El* and *La* Business, based on the worker's gender.

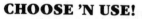

CHOOSE 'N USE!

- *¿Quién es...?*   Who is the... (boss, chef, teacher, etc.)?
- *Quiere ser...*   He/She wants to be a...(writer, farmer, lawyer, etc.).
- *...es excelente.*   The...(painter, mechanic, actress, etc.) is excellent.

HOT TIPS!

- Use Spanglish! *El overtime*; *La happy hour*; *El break*; *El lonche*.

- Demand it!
  ¡Hable con el jefe!
    Talk to the boss!
  ¡Cambie su cheque!
    Cash your check!
  ¡Tráigame la lista!
    Bring me the list!
  ¡Haga su horario!
    Make your schedule!

- Request it!
  Yo quisiera...
  I would like...
  Yo quisiera un trabajo.
    I would like a job.
  un negocio.
    a business.
  mis vacaciones.
    a vacation.
  un seguro.   insurance.
  más beneficios.   more benefits.
  el éxito.   success.
  una oportunidad.
    an opportunity.
  un puesto.   a position.
  una carrera.   a career.

- Threaten!
  ¡Voy a renunciar!
    I'm gonna quit!
  ¡Voy a salir!
    I'm gonna leave!

- Talk about him or her!
  Está...
  He's or She's...
  retirado(a)   retired
  contratado(a)   hired
  despedido(a)   fired

Trabajo, trabajo, trabajo...

There's really no way to present all the Spanish words related to *el trabajo* because we all hold different *trabajos*. The following is a *colección* of miscellaneous stuff. If you need to know the name of something specific at your workplace, ask a Spanish speaker for some help. (Remember: ***¿Qué es esto en español?*** is "What is this thing called in Spanish?")

Work on these words:

la agencia	agency	*la herramienta*	tool
el almacén	warehouse	*el horario*	schedule
el ayudante	helper	*la huelga*	strike
el cheque	check	*la junta*	meeting
el chofer	driver	*la lista*	list
la cita	appointment	*la máquina*	machine
la computadora	computer	*la máquina de*	
la conferencia	conference	*escribir*	typewriter
el contrato	contract	*el material*	material
la copiadora	copier	*la oficina*	office
el correo	mail	*el producto*	product
el entrenamiento	training	*el programa*	program
la entrevista	interview	*la reparación*	repair
la fábrica	factory	*la tarjeta*	time card
las formas	forms		

CHOOSE 'N USE!

- *¿Dónde está...?*   Where's the...(factory, meeting, etc.)?
- *Hay problemas con...*   There are problems with the... (typewriter, machine, etc.).
- *Me gusta...*   I like the...(driver, helper, etc.).
- *Necesito mi...*   I need my...(check, contract, etc.).

The Good, the Bad, and the Ugly

Describing people in Spanish is no different from describing places and things. As you've discovered you can rely on the Reversal Rule! Whenever you want to add a *description,* simply think *backwards.*

*Él es un **hombre grande.***
He is a **big man.**

> ### NOTE
> A different way to say the same thing is—*El hombre es grande.* And of course you'll need the *El* and *La* Business and the Once-and-for-All Rule:
> *El**las** son señorit**as** bonit**as**.*   They are pretty girls.

Now, why not delve into these describers!

grande big	*feo(a)* ugly	*simpático(a)* nice
chico(a) small	*bonito(a)* pretty	*extraño(a)* strange
bueno(a) good	*guapo(a)*	*fuerte* strong
malo(a) bad	handsome	*débil* weak
nuevo(a) new	*alto(a)* tall	*largo(a)* long
viejo(a) old	*flaco(a)* thin	*bajo(a)* short in
joven young	*gordo(a)* fat	height
perezoso(a) lazy	*loco(a)* crazy	*corto(a)* short in
trabajador(a)	*cuerdo(a)* sane	length
industrious		

HOT TIPS!

- *Descripción* words that start with *in*- usually refer to an opposite: *correcto* ▸ *incorrecto* (not correct)
- There are countless *descripciónes* which are easy to recall because *they're a lot like English:* favorito natural sincero moderno popular elegante terrible furioso *Be on the lookout* for "fakers." **Embarasada,** for example, does not mean "embarrassed" —it means pregnant!
- Now that you are putting two or more words together *on your own,* here's a suggestion: Be proud of yourself! Self-confidence builds from little successes. So whenever you describe —*relax* and just ramble on!
- For a complete *descripción,* do so as you would in *inglés.* The house is **big, red,** and **green.** *La casa es **grande, roja,** y **verde**.*

CHOOSE 'N USE!

- Usted no es muy…   You aren't very…(fat, old, etc.).
- Él es…, …, y…   He's…, (handsome, etc.), …, (tall, etc.), and…(nice).
- ¿Kim es…o…?   Is Kim…(lazy, etc.) or…(industrious)?
- Use these "little words" to elaborate:

más grande.   bigger
lo más grande.   biggest
tan grande *cómo…*   as big as…

Él es
He's

un poco a little
muy very
demasiado too
tan so

lento
slow

Más Descripciónes!

tonto(a)	dumb	*moreno(a)*	dark-haired
inteligente	smart	*pelirrojo(a)*	red-headed
brillante	bright	*calvo(a)*	bald
sucio(a)	dirty	*duro(a)*	hard
limpio(a)	clean	*blando(a)*	soft
lento(a)	slow	*rico(a)*	rich
rápido(a)	fast	*pobre*	poor
vacío(a)	empty	*valiente*	brave
lleno(a)	full	*cobarde*	cowardly
claro(a)	light	*interesante*	interesting
oscuro(a)	dark	*peligroso(a)*	dangerous
mayor	older	*roto(a)*	broken
menor	younger	*ancho(a)*	wide
fácil	easy	*estrecho(a)*	narrow
difícil	difficult	*suave*	smooth
barato(a)	inexpensive	*rasposo(a)*	rough
caro(a)	expensive	*famoso(a)*	famous
frío(a)	cold	*equivocado(a)*	wrong
caliente	hot to touch	*disponible*	available
picante	hot to taste	*maravilloso(a)*	marvelous
rubio(a)	blond	*perdido(a)*	lost

CHOOSE 'N USE!

- *Marco no es…*   Marco isn't…(rich, bald, old, etc.).
- *Mi carro parece…*   My car seems…(full, slow, dirty, etc.).
- *Quiero algo…*   I want something…(dark, soft, etc.).

6

CHAPTER *SEIS*

Las cosas

(Things)

"*Mi casa es su casa*"

As with all new words, it's best to learn these through "experience." Have a friend or another person command you to *move, point, pick up, carry,* or just *touch* the following common household objects:

Mueva...
Move...

Señale...
Point to...

Recoja...
Pick up...

Toque...
Touch...

Mire...
Look at...

Limpie...
Clean...

el sofá

el sillón

la lámpara

la silla

el televisor

el estereo

la pintura

la mesa

la puerta

el teléfono

la tina

el librero

la chimenea

la estufa

el refrigerador

el excusado

el lavabo

el reloj

el tocador

CHOOSE 'N USE!
- *...está quebrado(a).*   The...(lamp, refrigerator, etc.) is broken.
- *No puedo encontrar...*   I can't find the...(table, chair, etc.).
- *¿Cuánto cuesta...?*   How much is the...(stereo, stove, etc.)?

¡Más cosas en la casa!
la alfombra   rug
la aspiradora   vacuum cleaner
los cajones   drawers
el cesto de basura   trash can
las cortinas   curtains
los gabinetes   cabinets
la lavadora   washer
la licuadora   blender
el ropero   closet
la secadora   dryer
el tostador   toaster
el trapeador   mop
los trastes   dishes

Más aún (More still)
la almohada   pillow
el balde   bucket
la cobija   blanket
la escoba   broom
el espejo   mirror
el jabón   soap
la olla   pot
la plancha   iron
la regadera   shower
la sábana   sheet
el sartén   pan
la toalla   towel

HOT TIP!

Lots of household objects can be said in English and are easier if left untranslated! (Discover more on your own!)

el switch
el microwave
los CD's
los speakers
el VCR

CHOOSE 'N USE!
- *No tiene un/una...*   It doesn't have a...(cabinet, closet, etc.).
- *No me gusta el color de...*   I don't like the color of the...(rugs, curtains, etc.).

¿Dónde está?

Next time you can't find what you're looking for around *la casa,* send out a search party *en español!*

Here are a few places where it's most likely to be found.

Está en...
It's in (on, *or* at) the...

la recámara	bedroom	*el desván*	attic
las escaleras	stairs	*el baño*	bathroom
el sótano	basement	*el césped*	grass, lawn
el pasillo	hallway	*la cocina*	kitchen
la sala	living room	*el jardín*	garden
el comedor	dining room	*el garaje*	garage

Vocabulario especial

Voy a comprar...
I'm going to buy...

No tengo...
I don't have...

¿Puede Ud. reparar...?
Can you repair...?

el apartamento   apartment
el aire acondicionado
   air conditioning
las llaves   keys
la electricidad   electricity
los muebles   furniture
los enchufes   outlets
el portón   gate
el condominio   condominium
la calefacción   heating
las cerraduras   locks
la tubería   plumbing
las luces   lights
la cerca   fence
el timbre   doorbell

CHOOSE 'N USE!

- *Voy a buscar...* I'm going to look for...(furniture, locks etc.).
- *No tengo un/una...* I don't have a...(basement, attic, etc.).
- *¿Puede reparar...?* Can you repair...(the plumbing, stairs, etc.)?

Las herramientas (Tools)

los alicates pliers
el clavo nail
el destornillador screwdriver
la escalera ladder
la manguera hose
el martillo hammer
la pala shovel
el rastrillo rake
el serrucho saw
las tijeras scissors
el tornillo screw

Los materiales (Materials)

el alambre wire
el asfalto asphalt
la baldosa floor tile
el cartón cardboard
el cemento cement
la goma rubber
el ladrillo brick
la madera wood
la piedra stone
el plástico plastic
la tela cloth

HOT TIP!

Try these wonderful
one-liners.
Se me perdió. I lost it.
Se me olvidó. I forgot it.
Se me quebró. I broke it.

La vida en la ciudad grande
(Life in the big city)

Spanish fills our cities,…so let's leave the comfy confines of **la casa** and head into town. Walk, ride, or drive around *pointing* and *naming* things. (If you're caught talking to yourself, *don't stop!* It'll be too hard to explain.)

Los edificios (Buildings)
el banco   bank
la biblioteca   library
el cine   movies
el correo   post office
el departamento de bomberos
   fire department
la escuela   school
la estación de policía   police
   station
la fábrica   factory
la farmacia   pharmacy
la gasolinera   gas station
el hospital   hospital
la iglesia   church
el museo   museum
la oficina   office
el restaurante   restaurant
el supermercado   supermarket
la tienda   store

Los lugares y sitios
(Places and sites)
el aeropuerto   airport
la banqueta   sidewalk
el barrio or *la*
   colonia   neighborhood
la calle   street
el camino   road
la carretera   highway
el centro   downtown
la comunidad   community
la cuadra   city block
el elevador   elevator
la esquina   corner
el metro   subway
el parque   park
el piso   floor
el pueblo   town
el puente   bridge

CHOOSE 'N USE!

- *¿Sabe dónde está...?*   Do you know where the...(museum, bank, etc.) is?
- *...está cerca de...*   The...(church, etc.) is near the...(school, etc.).
- *Espéreme Ud. en...*   Wait for me at the...(subway, corner, etc.).

La transportación
(Transportation)

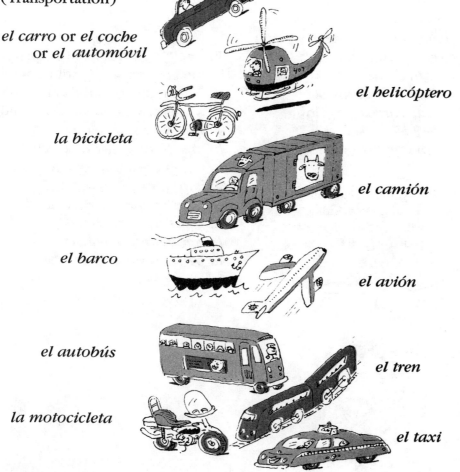

el carro or *el coche* or *el automóvil*

el helicóptero

la bicicleta

el camión

el barco

el avión

el autobús

el tren

la motocicleta

el taxi

CHOOSE 'N USE!

- *¿Va por...o...?*   Are you going by...(taxi, etc.) or...(train, etc.)?
- *No me gusta viajar por...*   I don't like traveling by...(airplane, etc.).
- *Busco...*   I'm looking for the...(bus, etc.).

Más City Life

la piscina	pool
el rascacielos	skyscraper
el cementerio	cemetary
el circo	circus
la cantina	bar
las afueras	outskirts
el lote de carros	car lot
el zoológico	zoo
el campamento	campgrounds

There is a little piece of language—***ería***—(pronounced air-EE-ah) that is found *at the end* of words which name *stores* and *shops.* Watch the pattern!

*la tortill**ería***	tortilla factory
*la muebl**ería***	furniture store
*la zapat**ería***	shoe store
*la carnic**ería***	meat market
*la joy**ería***	jewelry store
*la panad**ería***	bakery
*la peluqu**ería***	barber shop

As you travelers can see, the ***ería*** ending will work wonders for you as you're finding your way around *la ciudad grande.*

HOT TIPS!

• You may need these:
Las direcciones
N *(Norte)*
O *(Oeste)*
E *(Este)*
S *(Sur)*

• And fill out that form:
el condado
(county) _____
el estado
(state) _____
el país
(country) _____

307-30-5552

8038 B

8030 B

4 00 004

Sally Eagles 737-8023

Back to Nature

Let's get out of town for a while! But before we take off, why don't we "handle" a few of nature's little wonders that are within "reach"— right outside the door! And as we do with all new words of objects— let's *touch 'n talk.*

La naturaleza
(Nature)

el *árbol*   tree
el *arbusto*   bush
la *arena*   sand
la *flor*   flower
la *hierba*   grass
la *hoja*   leaf
el *lodo*   mud
el *palo*   stick
la *piedra*   rock
la *planta*   plant
el *polvo*   dust
la *rama*   branch
la *semilla*   seed

Los insectos
(Insects)

la *abeja*   bee
la *araña*   spider
la *hormiga*   ant
la *mosca*   fly

Los animales
(Animals)

Los domésticos
(the "domestic ones")
el caballo   horse
el chivo   goat
el gato   cat
la oveja   sheep
el pájaro   bird
el pato   duck
el perro   dog
el pez   fish
el pollo   chicken
el puerco   pig
el ratón   mouse
la vaca   cow

> Sometimes, animals aren't so easy to "handle," but have fun anyway!

Los salvajes
(the "wild ones"):
el camello   camel
la cebra   zebra
el elefante   elephant
el hipopótamo
   hippopotamus
la jirafa   giraffe
el león   lion
el mono   monkey
el oso   bear
el rinoceronte
   rhinoceros
el tigre   tiger
el venado   deer
la víbora   snake

CHOOSE 'N USE!

- *Hay...allí.*   There's...(a flower, a goat, etc.) over there.
- *¿Tiene...?*   Does it have...(bushes, chickens, etc.)?
- *No me gusta...*   I don't like...(mud, spiders, etc.).
- *¿Ha visto...?*   Have you seen the...(rock, camel, etc.)?
- *...es mi favorito.* The...(tiger, tree, etc.) is my favorite.

- *...no es peligroso(a).* The...(zebra, etc.) isn't dangerous.
- *...come mucho.* The...(bear, lion, etc.) eats a lot.
- *...es inteligente.* The...(monkey, dog, etc.) is smart.
- *...vive en la selva.* The...(hippopotamus, etc.) lives in the jungle.

Now let our words head for

el campo

(the countryside):

el bosque   forest
el cerro   hill
la costa   coast
el desierto   desert
el lago   lake
el mar   sea
la montaña   mountain

el océano   ocean
el rancho   ranch
el río   river
la selva   jungle
el valle   valley

CHOOSE 'N USE!

- *...es maravilloso(a).* The...(ranch, coast, etc.) is marvelous.

- *Ellos viven en...*   They live in the...(valley, ocean, etc.).
- *¡Vamos a...!*   Let's go to the...(lake, desert, etc.)!

"I'm Hungry" (*Tengo hambre*)

Food words, too, may differ slightly from *región* to *región*, but don't get nervous; instead, eat and ask! The words that follow can be used safely everywhere!

La comida

(Food!)

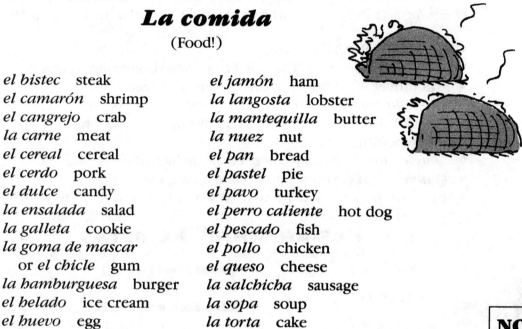

el bistec steak	*el jamón* ham
el camarón shrimp	*la langosta* lobster
el cangrejo crab	*la mantequilla* butter
la carne meat	*la nuez* nut
el cereal cereal	*el pan* bread
el cerdo pork	*el pastel* pie
el dulce candy	*el pavo* turkey
la ensalada salad	*el perro caliente* hot dog
la galleta cookie	*el pescado* fish
la goma de mascar	*el pollo* chicken
or *el chicle* gum	*el queso* cheese
la hamburguesa burger	*la salchicha* sausage
el helado ice cream	*la sopa* soup
el huevo egg	*la torta* cake

> **NOTE**
> Try to "mumble" these words before you *dig in!*

Las frutas

(Fruit)

la cereza cherry	*la naranja* orange
la fresa strawberry	*el plátano* banana
el limón lemon	*la toronja* grapefruit
la manzana apple	*la uva* grape

Las legumbres
(Vegetables)

la cebolla onion	*la lechuga* lettuce
la col or *el repollo* cabbage	*el maíz* corn
el guisante or *chícharo* pea	*la patata* or
la judía verde or *el ejote*	*papa* potato
green bean	*la zanahoria* carrot

La cocina

(Kitchen)

la cafetera	coffee pot	*el florero*	vase	*el delantal*	apron
el cántaro	pitcher	*la receta*	recipe	*el mantel*	tablecloth

CHOOSE 'N USE!

- *La ensalada tiene...*   The salad has...(carrots, onions, etc.).
- *¡...es dulce!*   The...(corn, orange, etc.) is sweet!
- *No puedo comer...*   I can't eat...(lemons, strawberries, etc.).
- *¿Quisiera una...o...?*   Would you like a...(banana, etc.) or a...(grapefruit)?
- *...huele mal.*   The...(lettuce, etc.) smells bad.
- *¿Quiere...?*   Do you want a...(tablecloth, etc.)?
- *Voy a comprar...*   I'm going to buy a...(vase, etc.).

"Restaurante" Remarks

¡Qué...
How

deliciosa (or *sabrosa*)!
  delicious!
picante!   hot (to taste)!
caliente!   hot (to touch)!

Quisiera (I'd like)...
  or
Ella tiene (She has)...
  or
Tráigame (Bring me)...

algo de comer.   something to eat.
algo de beber.   something to drink.
el plato del día.   today's special.
el menú.   a menu.
más agua.   more water.

¿Está...
Is it...

crudo(a)?   raw?
cocido(a)?   cooked?
frito(a)?   fried?
fresco(a)?   fresh?
maduro(a)?   ripe?
podrido(a)?   rotten?

Now munch on these helpful tidbits:
Estoy en dieta.   I'm on a diet.
Para comer aquí.   To eat here.
Para llevar.   To go.
Quiero ordenar.   I want to order.
las comidas   The meals
el desayuno   breakfast
el almuerzo   lunch
la cena   dinner

Eat these words up:

la botella   bottle
la camarera or *mesera*   waitress
el camarero or *mesero*   waiter
el cenicero   ashtray
el (la) cocinero(a)   cook
la cuchara   spoon
el cuchillo   knife
la cuenta   check
la lata   can
el plato   plate
el postre   dessert
la propina   tip
la servilleta   napkin
la taza   cup
el tenedor   fork
el vaso   glass

Tengo sed

(I'm thirsty)
el batido   milk shake
la bebida   a drink
el café   coffee
el café descafeinado
    decaffeinated coffee
la cerveza   beer
el hielo   ice
el jugo   juice
la leche   milk
la limonada   lemonade
el refresco   refreshment
la sangría   wine &
    fruit juice
la soda   soft drink
el té   tea
el vino   wine

Los sabores

(Flavors)
Está…
It's…
dulce.   sweet.
amargo(a).   bitter.
agrio(a).   sour.
seco(a).   dry.
salado(a).   salty.

Los ingredientes

(Ingredients)
el aceite   oil   *la harina*   flour
el ajo   garlic   *la miel*   honey
el arroz   rice   *la mostaza*   mustard
el azúcar   sugar   *la pimienta*   pepper
el caldo   broth   *la sal*   salt
la crema   cream   *la salsa*   sauce

CHOOSE 'N USE!

- *Necesito…*   I need the…(waiter, napkin, etc.).
- *…está sucio (a).*   The…(glass, fork, etc.) is dirty.
- *Se me cayó…*   I dropped the…(ashtray, cup, etc.).
- *Necesita más…*   It needs more…(sauce, mustard, etc.).
- *Hay demasiado(a)…*   There's too much…(salt, garlic, etc.).
- *No bebo…*   I don't drink…(wine, juice, etc.).
- *¿Quiere Ud.…o…?*   Do you want…(coffee) or…(tea)?
- *…está horrible.*   The…(drink, etc.) is horrible.

HOT TIP!

Use **mucho** and **poco** for a **large** and **small** "amount." **Muchos** and **pocos** are for **many** and **a few!**

"What are You Wearing?"
(¿Qué lleva?)

...Get dressed in Spanish! The next time you're putting something on, name it *en español!*

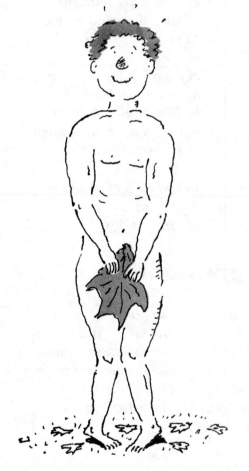

el abrigo   overcoat
la bata de baño   bathrobe
la blusa   blouse
las botas   boots
la bufanda   scarf
los calcetines   socks
los calzoncillos   shorts
la camisa   shirt
la camiseta   T-shirt
la chaqueta   jacket
el cinturón   belt
la corbata   tie
la falda   skirt
la gorra   cap
los guantes   gloves
el impermeable   raincoat
las medias   stockings
los pantalones   pants
la pijama   pajamas
la ropa interior
   underwear
el saco   sportscoat
el sombrero   hat
las sudaderas   sweatsuit
el suéter   sweater
los tenis   tennis shoes
el traje   suit
el traje de baño   bathing
   suit
el vestido   dress
las zapatillas   slippers
los zapatos   shoes

CHOOSE 'N USE!

- *¿Dónde compró Ud....?*
  Where did you buy the…(jacket, shirt, etc.)?
- *Me gusta el color de…*
  I like the color of the…(blouse, pants, etc.).
- *Necesito…*   I need the…(slippers, suit, etc.).
- *¿Cuánto cuesta…?*   How much is the…(dress, overcoat, etc.)?
- *…son muy viejos.*   The…(shoes, shorts, etc.) are very old.

Lavar la ropa
(Washing clothes)

"The cleaners" are *los limpiadores*
"Dirty laundry" is *la ropa sucia*
"Detergent" is *el detergente*
"Stain" is *la mancha*
"Bleach" is *el blanqueador*
"Hangers" are *los ganchos*
"Laundromat" is *la lavandería*

HOT TIPS!

- Describe clothes with *los colores!*
- *Un par de* is "a pair of"
- You may hear *different words* used to name these things. *Who cares?* These will work fine!

"Let's Go Shopping"
¡Vamos de compras!

el dinero   money
el cheque   check
la tarjeta de crédito
    credit card

el cambio   change
la cuenta   bill
el cupón   coupon
el descuento   discount
el enganche   down payment
la ganga   bargain
la oferta   offer
el pago   payment
el precio   price
el recibo   receipt
la venta   sale

CHOOSE 'N USE!

- *Busco...*   I am looking for the...(sale, perfume, etc.).
- *Quisiera...*   I'd like the...(receipt, change, etc.).
- *¿Se vende...?*   Do you sell...(rings, combs, etc.)?
- *¿Dónde están...?*   Where are the...(suitcases, diamonds, etc.)?

La joyería

(Jewelry Store)

el anillo ring   los diamantes diamonds
los aretes earrings   las joyas jewels
el brazalete bracelet   el oro gold
el broche brooch   las perlas pearls
la cadena chain   la plata silver
el collar necklace   el reloj watch

Buyer's Babble!

¿Es todo?   Is that all?
¡Me gusta!   I like it!
¿Qué marca es?   What brand is it?
No me queda.   It doesn't fit.
Me quedo con ésto.   I'll take this.
¿Cuánto cuesta? (or ¿Cuánto vale?)   How much is it?
¿Cuánto pesa?   How much does it weigh?
Quiero probármelo.   I want to try it on.
Quiero cargarlo a mi cuenta.
  I want to charge it (to my account).

¿En qué puedo servirle?   Can I help you?
¿Algo más?   Something else?
¿Cuánto por ciento?   What percent?
Es gratis.   It's free.
Necesito un dependiente.   I need a clerk.
Quiero un(a) cajero(a).   I want a cashier.
¿Cuál departamento?   Which department?

Unas Extras

la bolsa   bag; purse
la caja   box
la cartera   wallet
el cepillo   brush
la cinta   ribbon
la maleta   suitcase
el maletín   briefcase
el maquillaje   make-up
la mochila   knapsack
el paraguas   umbrella
el peine   comb
el perfume   perfume

¿Cuál es su talla?

(What's your size?)

Uso un...
I take a...
chico   small
mediano   medium
grande   large
extra   X large

"Get into the Act!"

There's no better way to learn than by *doing*. That is why the best language programs include *commands* as a method to teach both *actions* as well as *objects*.

¡Cante la canción!
Sing the song!
¡Saluden la bandera!
Salute the flag!

Commands involve both the speaker and the listener.

With friends and family, take turns giving each other *mandatos* (commands). Select common objects, and using the commands below, act them out! (they're great for work or play!)

Mueva (Move)
Lleve (Carry)
Levante (Raise)
Prenda (Turn on)
Traiga (Bring)
Toque (Touch)
Señale (Point to)
Baje (Lower)
Apague (Turn off)
Mire (Watch)

la televisión
(television)
or
esto
(this)
or
eso
(that)

¡Más mandatos!

Baile Dance	*Lea* Read	*Saque* Take out
Busque Look for	*Limpie* Clean	*Siga* Continue
Cante Sing	*Llame* Call	*Suba* Climb
Coma Eat	*Mande* Send	*Tome* Drink
Compre Buy	*Marque* Dial	*Vea* See
Corra Run	*Meta* Put inside;	*Venda* Sell
Escriba Write	*Pida* Ask for	*Venga* Come
Escuche Listen	*Quite* Take away	
Firme Sign	*Regrese* Return	
Lave Wash	*Repita* Repeat	

Let's make a *mandato!*

A simple approach to forming a command in Spanish requires knowledge of the three different action word (verb) endings. The endings are:

> **ar** as in *hablar*   to speak
> **er** as in *comer*   to eat
> **ir** as in *escribir*   to write

To make a *mandato,* drop the last two letters of the infinitive ("to") form and replace them as follows:

> **ar** → **e**
> *hablar* → *¡Hable!*   Speak!
>
> **er** → **a**
> *comer* → *¡Coma!*   Eat!
>
> **ir** → **a**
> *escribir* → *¡Escriba!*   Write!

But **beware**! Some verbs are weird and simply have to be memorized.

> *ir* → *¡Vaya!*   Go!
> *venir* → *¡Venga!*   Come!
> *decir* → *¡Diga!*   Speak!

- Because commands are exchanged so often between friends, you may hear folks using the *tú* (or informal) form of the action words. Don't get excited. Here are a few common "informal" commands:
  ¡Ven!   Come here!
  ¡Véte!   Go away!
  ¡Díme!   Tell me!
  ¡Espérate!   Wait!
  ¡Cállate!   Shut up!
  ¡Llámame!   Call me!
- Use the previously listed commands for now, and don't worry about forming your own yet. You'll get the idea with practice!
- To tell someone *not* to do something, just put **no** in front of the command!
- When you can't remember the name of an object, use **esto** for "this thing" or **eso** for "that thing."
- You can always get your idea across by simply using the basic action (verb) form preceded by *favor de* (please).
  Favor de hablar.
  Please speak.
  Favor de seguir.
  Please continue.
- Start now by following these simple commands!
  ¡Toque el libro!
  Touch the book!
  ¡Escriba su nombre!
  Write your name!
  ¡Baile la Bamba!
  Dance the Bamba!

Los Mighty *Mandatos!*

Here are some common commands that are almost always given alone, and they work well *all by themselves!* (They are actually two words rolled into one.)

HOT TIPS!

- Remember—inside each command is an *action word!* (Using commands will help you learn the Spanish verbs.)
- As you "command" and "order folks around," *be nice!* Add *por favor* (please) and *gracias* (thanks). And *smile!*
- Watch out for those (accent) marks! That part of the word must be said louder!
- Don't try to figure out *se, lo, me,* and the other "little endings." You'll get their meanings as you speak more. So for now, practice each command as you did the one-liners.
- Pick one command to play with each day! They're best for commanding *one person only!* To tell a *group* to do something, add an ***n*** to the action word: *¡Señalen* means "You guys, point!"

¡Agárrelo! Grab it!	*¡Dígame!* Tell me!
¡Cállese! Shut up!	*¡Espérese!* Wait!
¡Cálmese! Calm down!	*¡Hágalo!* Do it!
¡Créame! Believe me!	*¡Levántese!* Stand up!
¡Cuídese! Take care of yourself!	*¡Párese!* Stop!
¡Déjelo! Leave it alone!	*¡Pregúntele!* Ask him or her!
¡Démelo! Give it to me!	*¡Recójalo!* Pick it up!
¡Despiértese! Wake up!	*¡Siéntese!* Sit down!
	¡Vámonos! Let's go!

As you speak, help convey meaning through facial expressions and body language.

7

CHAPTER *SIETE*

¡Acción!
(Action!)

Un Anuncio Importante

You are about to enter the next level of proficiency in Spanish.

Please read:

- This chapter introduces Spanish action words or verbs. Do not be afraid! There is no "conjugating." Instead, general suggestions are made, and *practical* action word lists are presented here. But you still have to pay attention. Believe it or not, this stuff is what *makes Spanish really work!*

- As always, *mistakes are good,* so don't hold back. Keep a positive attitude, and do the best you can. Don't worry about every word! Use only what you need.

NOTE

Spanish is easy! Most action words have the same base form. This means that all you have to do to understand action words is focus on the *first part* of the word. Here's how it works:

First, take a typical action, like "to work" (*trabajar*). Now let's see what the base **trabaj-** can do!

¡Trabaj-en! (Work!)

¡Trabaj-aron! (They worked!)

¡Trabaj-amos! (We work!)

¡Trabaj-ando! (Working!)

¡Trabaj-aba! (I used to work!)

¡Trabaj-ara! (I would work!)

Basics in Action

There are only three action word endings. The basic word-forms end in **-ar, -er** or **-ir**. That's it. Action words can be used all by themselves. You won't always be correct, but people will still understand. To get "extensive training" in *action words* (verbs), buy a textbook, or take a class. But for simple communication, try to pick up on the vocabulary and tips that follow.

A Big Step Toward Fluency

Words and one-liners are great, if you like to keep things short. But to make a Spanish conversation last, sooner or later you'll need the "to be" words, *estar* and *ser* (**"The Big 8"**).

Remember: you can drop the *quién* words if you like.

Estar

It seems GRINGOS tend to pick up the following words right away:

Yo	***estoy***	I **am**
Usted		You **are**
Él	***está***	He **is**
Ella		She **is**
(Una cosa)		It **is**
Ustedes		You guys **are**
Ellos	***están***	They **are**
Ellas		They **are**
(Dos or *más cosas)*		They **are**
Nosotros(as)	***estamos***	We **are**

Chances are you're already using these action words! If not, here it is in capsule form: ***Estar*** can mean **am, is** or **are** when talking about:
Condition
*¿Cómo **está** usted?*
or
Location
*¿Dónde **está** María?*

See how all forms begin the same?

Est	–	*oy*
Est	–	*á*
Est	–	*án*
Est	–	*amos*

Knowing these **four** magic words will make the difference!

A closer look at *estar*

- *Estás* is used with *tú.* (It means "You are" among friends or family members.)
- *Esta* without the accent mark (´) means "This." *Esta es una mesa.* This is a table.
- "Think" a bit before you use them. Put your words together just as you do in *inglés!*
  I am happy. → *Yo **estoy** contento.* **(condition)**
  The chair **is** over there. → *La silla **está** allí.* **(location)**
- Check back on *"Es versus Está"!* .

Take *un momento* to read the next few pages with care!

Ser

The other "to be" word is ***ser*** and it's BIG-TIME!

See how weird it is! You'll just have to watch closely. Trust me. It's worth it!

soy	I'm
es	you're, he's, she's, it's
son	they're, you guys are
somos	we're

Instead of location or condition *ser* words relate to:

- *the time*   • *occupation*
- *names*   • *nationality*
- *origin*   • *description*

Check out these examples:

> *Soy Tony.*   *Es italiano.*   *Somos dentistas.*
> *Es de oro.*   *Son amigos.*
> *Son las dos.*   *Es grande.*   *Soy de Los Angeles.*
> *Es de día.*   *Es una enchilada.*
> *Son para Susana y Roberto.*

To Be or Not To Be

Estar
For location and condition (at this moment).

Ser
For everything else!

¡Atención!

Look closely amigos—you've only got **eight words** to remember! and *they don't ever change.*

estoy   soy

está   es

están   son

estamos   somos

HOT TIPS!

- To ask questions, use statements— simply add question marks before and after.
  María es bonita.
  Mary is pretty.
  ¿María es bonita?
  Is Mary pretty?
- Or, if you'd like, the subject in question can be moved to the end:
  ¿Es bonita María?
  (Word order in Spanish won't really hurt the message.)

Notice the *difference!*

Estar

Yo **estoy aquí.**   I'm here.
Ella **está** *bien.*   She's fine.
Mis amigos **están** *ocupados.*   My friends are busy.
Nosotros **estamos** *trabajando.*   We're working.

Ser

Yo **soy** *Tony.*   I'm Tony.
Ella **es** *cubana.*   She's Cuban.
Mis amigos **son** *altos.*   My friends are tall.
Nosotros **somos** *dentistas.*   We're dentists.

DO IT NOW!

By "fooling around" with these ASAP, gringos can immediately begin sending complete messages. Back up a few pages and reread. You'll be amazed at how much better your Spanish will be!

TRY SOME!

1. *Tony* **está** *en la casa.*
2. *Ellos* **son** *inteligentes.*
3. *Yo* **estoy** *bien.*
4. **Somos** *cubanos.*
5. **Estamos** *muy contentos.*
6. **Soy** *el presidente.*
7. _____
8. _____
9. _____
10. _____

Just Say No!

What is truly *magnífico* about *español* is that there are so many shortcuts to success! As we've seen, to say *"not"* in Spanish, it's *no* big deal. Do *nothing* more than place a *no* in front of whatever you're trying to say.

La rata es muy grande.
La rata no es muy grande.

And *no* matter how complex the action, to say "not" just say, *no*!

Ella no quiere leer libros y escribir ejercicios.
(She does not want to read books and write exercises!)

Take a second to scan these *muy* useful *no-no's:*

 No . . .

hay.	There **isn't** or **aren't** any.
importa.	It's **not** important.
me interesa.	**I'm** not interested.
le haga caso.	**Don't** pay any attention.
me dí cuenta.	I **didn't** realize.
lo aguanto.	I **can't** stand it.
se preocupe.	**Don't** worry.
sabía.	I **didn't** know.
puede ser.	It **can't** be.
me gusta.	I **don't** like it.

Now, what can you learn about action words from these examples?

***No** puedo*	I can't.	***No** quiero*	I don't want…
***No** tengo*	I don't have…	***No** recuerdo*	I don't remember.
***No** veo*	I can't see.	***No** encuentro*	I can't find…
***No** necesito*	I don't need…		

HOT TIP!

In Spanish, you need a **double no**: *¿Está Juan?* — ***No, no** está.* (Is John there? No he is not.) For words like *nadie* (nobody), put ***No*** in front of verb: ***No** está nadie.* (Nobody is here.)

Let's *Tengo!*

Remember: you can delete the *quién words* if you like.

Here's another "power play" en *español*—and truly a *must* for the rookie. Whenever you'd like to talk about **who has** what, use the action word **tener** (to have).

tengo and *tiene* are great for requests and "chit-chat."
> ¿**Tiene** *cambio?*   Do you have change?
> **Tengo** *dos hermanos.*   I have two brothers.

Tenemos (**We** have) and **tienen** (**you guys** or **they** have) are also nice to know.

	TENER to have	
Yo **tengo** I **have**	*Ustedes*	
	Ellos **tienen** They, You **have**	
Usted	*Ellas*	
Ella **tiene** You, He, She **has**		
Él	*Nosotros tenemos* We have	

TENER can also mean *to be* in the following situations:

Tengo la culpa. I'm at fault.	*Tengo razón.* I'm right.
Tengo hambre. I'm hungry.	*Tengo frío.* I'm cold.
Tengo sed. I'm thirsty.	*Tengo calor.* I'm hot.
Tengo miedo. I'm scared.	*Tengo sueño.* I'm sleepy.
Tengo suerte. I'm in luck.	*Tengo 18 años.* I'm 18 years old.

See how these make great one-liners. And they all work with the other forms of **TENER** just as well:

> *Tenemos miedo.*   We're scared.
> ¿*Tiene frío?*   Are you cold?
> *Tienen hambre.*   They're hungry.

...Here you go! Make some of your own:

_____

_____

_____

"What Are You Doing?" (*¿Qué está haciendo?*)

Acción words in Spanish are usually learned in a predictable order. First, the commands are picked up along with the "to be" words, ***ser*** and ***estar***. Second come the action words referring to "now!" (I call this the **"-*ing*"** or **-*ndo*** form.) It's the easiest form to remember and to use. All that's needed is an *acción* word. To say "talking" for example, simply change *hablar* (talk) to *hablando*:

$$hablar \rightarrow habla\textbf{ndo}$$
$$(talk) \qquad (talk\textbf{ing})$$

The **-*ndo*** replaces the **-*r***. All Spanish action words end in *-r,* so the *-ndo* or *-ing* form is *muy simple!*

- *trabajar* trabaja**ndo**
  work   work**ing**

- *comprar* compra**ndo**
  buy   buy**ing**

- *manejar* maneja**ndo**
  drive   driv**ing**

NOTE

Some *acción* words end in **-*er*** or **-*ir*** so you have to change the ending to **-*iendo*** instead of **-*ando***:

- *comer*   comie**ndo**
  eat   eating

- *escribir*   escribie**ndo**
  write   writing

HOT TIPS!

- Relax! All you need to remember is either ***ando*** or ***iendo***.
- And to "complete" your message, just put the *estar* words in front: "Maria **is** working." becomes *María* **está** *trabajando.*

Onward with...*ndo*

The key to *real* fluency is to acquire as many *acción words as* possible. Try "fooling around" with these words. First, "-ing" 'em with **-ando** or **-iendo**! Then use them to make statements.

correr (run)   *Ellos están corr**iendo**.*   They're running.
caminar (walk) *Estoy camin**ando**.*   I'm walking.
salir (leave)   *El tren está sal**iendo**.*   The train is leaving.

abrir	open	*jugar*	play	*pagar*	pay
aprender	learn	*limpiar*	clean	*poner*	put
beber	drink	*lavar*	wash	*tirar*	throw
besar	kiss	*llegar*	arrive	*vender*	sell
cerrar	close	*llevar*	carry	*viajar*	travel
empujar	push	*llorar*	cry	*volver*	return
jalar	pull	*mostrar*	show		

HOT TIPS!

- Many action words are *muy* easy to remember.
  flotar float
  plantar plant
  visitar visit
  controlar control
  And some are easier to learn combined with other words
  marcar el número dial the number
  llamar por teléfono call by phone
  mirar televisión watch TV
- **Be careful!** A few action words are not what they seem!
  pretender to court someone
  embarazar to impregnate
  And a few of these words change a little when you "*-ndo.*"
  leer (read) becomes *leyendo* (reading)
  dormir (sleep) becomes *durmiendo* (sleeping)
  decir (say) becomes *diciendo* (saying)
- When "*-ndo*-ing," are you putting *estoy, está, están,* and *estamos* "in front"?

Ready, Set...

At this stage of the guidebook, most of you have already started to race forward, constantly in search of *más palabras de acción.*
You have found that knowing how to use the *-ndo* form changes everything. After jabbering a couple of *acciones,* along with some *vocabulario básico,* you have begun to feel like a native speaker. However, before you volunteer as a tour guide, let's first take a look at a few more secrets to understanding those action words!

Beyond...*ndo*

There's no way that beginning "Spanish-speakers" can pick up all the different action word forms right away. However, after the "*-ndo*'s," it is possible to "shortcut" your way through some of the other grammar junk.

Here is a *grupo* of goodies that will help! You can put these phrases **in front of** action words.

Hay que (One must)...   *trabajar.* (work.)
Me gusta (I like)...   *comer.* (eat.)
Favor de (Please)...   *escribir.* (write.)
Acabo de (I have just finished)...
Tengo que (I have to)...
Debo (I should)...
Prefiero (I prefer to)...
Necesito (I need to)...
Puedo (I can)...
Deseo (I wish to)...
Quiero (I want to)...
Quisiera (I'd like to)...

HOT TIP!

You'll be hearing folks add *-ado* or *-ido* to action words instead of *-ndo*. Don't worry about it. It usually means that the action has been completed. *¿Entendido? (Understood?)* Remember: Action words have only three basic endings, (**-ar, -er,** and **-ir).**

Se

A small number of *palabras de acción* have **se** attached. Don't get excited! It simply means that the action is one that *we do to ourselves.* Here's how they work.

lavar is "to wash."

lavarse means "to wash oneself." To "*-ndo,*" say— *lavándose* (washing oneself)

Add *estar* and it's, *Él está lavándose.* (He's washing himself.)

Check out some *más!*

- *acostarse*   lie down
  Nosotros estamos acostándonos.   We're ly**ing** down.
- *bañarse*   bathe oneself
  Ella está bañándose.   She's tak**ing a bath.**
- *cepillarse*   brush one's hair
  Yo estoy cepillándome.   I'm brush**ing** my hair.
- *levantarse*   raise oneself up
  Yo estoy levantándome.   I'm gett**ing** up.
- *peinarse*   comb one's hair
  Juan está peinándose.   John's comb**ing** his hair.
- *sentarse*   sit down
  Ellos están sentándose.   They're sitt**ing** down.

Here's what all these words look like together!

lavarse   wash oneself

*Estoy lavándo**me***	*Está lavándo**se***
*Están lavándo**se***	*Estamos lavándo**nos***

NOTE
- To say "I'm doing it to myself," use *me.*
- To say "We're doing it to ourselves," use *nos.*

CHOOSE 'N USE!

- *¿Quién está...?*   Who is...(bathing, standing up, etc.)?
- *Estoy...ahora mismo.*   I am (lying down, etc.) right now.
- *Estamos...y...*   We are...(combing) and...(brushing our hair).

lo, la le, les, me, nos

Understanding these little pieces of Spanish is easier than using them correctly. So for now, here's what they mean *when used with* action words!

lo; la   it
le   you, him, her
les   you guys, them
me   me
nos   us

Here's what they look like in normal conversation:

Me lo dijo.   He told it to me.
Lo tengo.   I have it.
Nos escribe.   He writes to us.
Pregúntele.   Ask him.

And notice how they usually require the "Reversal Rule"!

La   *La estoy limpiando.*   I am cleaning it.
Lo   *Juan lo está haciendo.*   Juan is doing it.
Le   *Le están escribiendo.*   They are writing you (or him, her).
Les   *Les estamos diciendo.*   We are telling them.
Me   *María me está besando.*   Maria is kissing me.
Nos   *Ella nos está enseñando.*   She is teaching us.

This is not easy. Even native Spanish speakers sometimes have problems with these little devils! But don't let them bother you—for now, just be aware of their general meaning and importance.

Here are more of those practical, everyday *palabras de acción* you **really can use** all the time!

Don't forget!
-er, -ir = *iendo;*
-ar = *ando!*

adivinar	guess	*jugar*	play
ahorrar	save	*juntar*	join
amar	love	*montar*	ride
apostar	bet	*nadar*	swim
aprovechar	take advantage	*odiar*	hate
arreglar	arrange	*olvidar*	forget
asistir	attend	*perder*	lose
bailar	dance	*pesar*	weigh
buscar	look for	*pescar*	fish
cantar	sing	*platicar*	chat
celebrar	celebrate	*prestar*	lend
cocinar	cook	*probar*	try
contestar	answer	*quebrar*	break
cortar	cut	*quitar*	take away
dar	give	*recibir*	receive
desarollar	develop	*renunciar*	quit
descansar	rest	*reparar*	fix
desear	wish	*sobrevivir*	survive
disfrutar	enjoy	*soñar*	dream
empezar	begin	*subir*	climb
encontrar	find	*terminar*	finish
escuchar	listen	*tocar*	touch
evitar	avoid	*traducir*	translate
gastar	spend	*usar*	use
gritar	yell	*volar*	fly

HOT TIPS!

- It's very likely that you're going to hear many action words that *mean the same* as those listed here! Learn those, too—in case you're "in a bind."
- Some action words have two or more useful meanings: *ganar* (win, earn); *tomar* (take, drink); *hacer* (do, make); *pegar* (hit, stick); *dejar* (leave behind, allow); *pasar* (pass, happen).
- Most commonly used action words end in *-ar,* so use the "*-ando*'s" first!
- Don't worry about spellings now. Speak first!

CHOOSE 'N USE!
- *Mi amigo está...*   My friend is...(yelling, fishing, etc.).
- *Los niños están...*   The children are...(guessing, etc.).
- *Yo estoy...mucho.*   I am...(chatting, etc.) a lot.
- *Nosotros no estamos...*   We are not...(flying, riding, etc.).
- *¿Ustedes están...?*   Are you guys...(listening)?
- *El Sr. Gómez está...y...*   Mr. Gomez is...(swimming) and...(riding).

Las Acciones Locas

No doubt you have some questions about a few action words that don't seem to perform like the others. I call them *"las locas"* (the "crazies"). Let's take a look at a few of my favorites:

ir (to go)

What's *fantástico* about **ir** is that it tells:
- where you're **"going to"** and
- what you're **"going to"** do later

Learn these words:
Voy a (I'm "going to")…***México***
Va a (You're, He's, She's "going to")…***mi casa.***
Van a (You guys, They are "going to")…***trabajar.***
Vamos a (We're "going to")…***comer.***

Saber and conocer (To know)

Saber and *conocer* both mean to know, but here's how they differ:
saber *(sé, sabe, saben, sabemos)* means "to know something."
conocer *(conozco, conoce, conocen, conocemos)* means "to know someone."

Yo **sé** *mucho español.*   I know a lot of Spanish.
Yo **conozco** *a muchas personas.*   I know a lot of people.

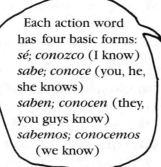

Each action word has four basic forms:
sé; conozco (I know)
sabe; conoce (you, he, she knows)
saben; conocen (they, you guys know)
sabemos; conocemos (we know)

HOT TIPS!

- Apply **ir a** to talk about the "future"! *¡Usted **va a** hablar español!* You're gonna speak Spanish! *¡María **va a** cocinar mañana!* Mary's gonna cook tomorrow! *¡Nosotros **vamos a** ir luego!* We're gonna go later!
- It might be a good idea to learn the **tú** or informal ways to say "you know." (saber) *sabe**s*** *Tú sabe**s** hablar español.* **You know** how to speak Spanish. (conocer) *conoce**s*** *¿Tú conoce**s** a María?* Do **you know** Maria?
- Notice how you need to say **a** after *conocer* and many other action words when referring to people.

"What happened?" (¿Qué pasó?)

There are tons more. Buy a Spanish textbook if you want to learn *más!*

Unfortunately, in Spanish, telling someone about previous events can be done several ways, depending upon your meaning. These are learned gradually when exposed consistently to lots of *español.* So, for the *momento,* let's view a few common "past" words that can help you ASAP!

> *Dijo*   said (you, he, she)
> *Fue*   went (you, he, she)
> *Comí*   ate (I)
> *Tenía*   used to have (I, you, he, she)
> *Iba*   was going (I, he, she); were going (you)

Estaba is the *"was"* word! To talk about past action.
*¿Qué est**aba** haciendo?*   What *were* you doing?
Try these words:

Yo	***estaba***	I was
Usted	***estaba***	You were
Ella	***estaba***	She was
Él	***estaba***	He was
Ellos	***estaban***	They were
Ustedes	***estaban***	You guys were
Nosotros	***estábamos***	We were

NOTE

• They go great with the *-ndo*'s. Also there are only three words to recall; not four!
• **Beware!** There are other **"was"** words.
• Believe me, this **"was" word** will get you going. You can finally start talking about the past!
Ella estaba aquí ayer.   She **was** here yesterday.
Estábamos trabajando anoche.   We **were** working last night.
Yo no estaba en casa.   I **wasn't** home.
¿Estaban jugando ellos?   **Were** they playing?

CHOOSE 'N USE!

• *¿Conoce usted a…?*   Do you know…(Mary, Tom, etc.)?
• *Trabajo en….*   I work at the…(store, bank, etc.).
• *No estaban….*   They weren't…(working, eating, etc.).
• *Él no sabe….*   He doesn't know the…(name, number, etc.).
• *Fue a….*   He, She went to…(Japan, Europe, etc.).

Bueno, before we *"stop* the action," here's some helpful "inside info" on Spanish *acciones* y *actividades.*

• The worlds of Spanglish and slang have produced countless action words that can be heard daily, particularly in those areas of this country where lots of both Spanish and English are spoken. Try some! (Many sound the same in English.) And of course, *make sure you understand what you're saying.* Use your *best* judgment!

- Read *español*. This is perhaps one of the best ways to learn the various action word forms (tenses). You'll soon be picking up and using stuff that used to take GRINGOS years to learn!

- Notice that action words in *español* have the same form for **we!** No matter what you're trying to say, the (*we*) ending is **-mos.**

	so**mos.**	**We** are.
Nosotros...	baila**mos.**	**We** dance.
	comi**mos.**	**We** ate.

The "you guys" or "they" ending is also easy to remember. Listen for the **n**.

Ellos...	so**n.**	**They** are.
	baila**n.**	**They** dance.
Ustedes...	comiero**n.**	**You guys** ate!

These are only a couple of *muchos* patterns that remain consistent among Spanish action words. So pay attention! You are bound to discover many more.

- There's a unique set of words in Spanish that really go *bien* with the *palabras de acción.* They tell **"how** we do things." What's nice is they all end in **-mente.** (I call 'em the "-ly words." Notice how much they look like *inglés!)*

*breve***mente** briefly	*perfecta***mente** perfectly
*correcta***mente** correctly	*rápida***mente** rapidly
*efectiva***mente** effectively	*sincera***mente** sincerely
*inmediata***mente** immediately	*usual***mente** usually

And here's how they work:
Juan está trabajando **rápidamente.**   Juan's working rapidly.
Estoy hablando **sinceramente.**   I'm talking sincerely.
Estamos jugando **perfectamente.**   We're playing perfectly.
Usualmente *no hay problemas.*   Usually, there aren't any problems.

8

CHAPTER *OCHO*
Los detalles
(Details)

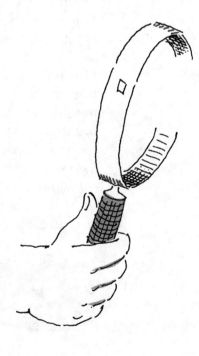

Tell Me When!

We've become familiar with some of these "when" words already. But now—with our knowledge of ¿Cuándo? (and some palabras básicas)—it's time to present the most popular words and phrases referring to **el tiempo.** (Recognize any of these one-liners?)

ahora   now; nowadays
ahorita   right now
a la madrugada   at dawn
al anochecer   at dusk
a la puesta del sol   at sunset
anoche   last night
anteayer   the day before yesterday
antes   before
apenas   just
a veces   sometimes
ayer   yesterday
cada día   each day
después   afterward
entonces   then
esta noche   tonight
hace dos años   two years ago
hasta   until
hoy   today
luego   later

mañana   tomorrow
mañana por la mañana   tomorrow morning
el mes pasado   last month
muchas veces   lots of times
nunca   never
pasado mañana   the day after tomorrow
pronto   soon
la próxima semana   next week
el próximo mes   next month
la semana pasada   last week
siempre   always
tarde   late
temprano   early
todavía   yet
todos los días   every day
una vez   once
un momento   a moment
un rato   awhile
ya   already

CHOOSE 'N USE!
- *Trabajo...*   I work...(today, always, etc.).
- *Estoy trabajando...*   I'm working...(right now, late, etc.).
- *Estaba trabajando...*   I was working...(yesterday, then, etc.).
- *He trabajado...*   I've worked...(before, every day, etc.).
- *Voy a trabajar...*   I'm going to work...(tomorrow, next month, etc.).

Tell Me Where!

Many "location" words were introduced earlier. The subsequent phrases and words allow us to express *exactly* where something (or someone) is located.

With these little beauties, you can answer almost any *¿Dónde?* question. They're OK alone, but they're better in sentences. (You'd be *lost* without them.)

abajo de down	*debajo de* under
adentro; dentro de inside	*desde* from
afuera; fuera de outside	*detrás de* behind
al fondo de at the bottom	*en* in, on, at
al lado de next to	*encima de* above
a lo largo de along	*enfrente de* in front of
alrededor de around	*entre* between
arriba de up	*hacia* towards
cerca de near	*lejos de* far from
contra against	*sobre* over

CHOOSE 'N USE!

- *Voy a ponerlo... las cajas.*   I'm going to put it...(inside, above, etc.) the boxes.
- *La oficina está... las tiendas.*   The office is...(near, next to, etc.) the stores.
- *El ratón está corriendo... ellos.*   The mouse is running... (toward, under, etc.) them.

Super "where" words!
cualquier parte   anywhere
por algún lugar   somewhere
por ningún lado   nowhere
por todas partes   everywhere

Here's how to "put together" these new words with others you've learned. (The word-joining process is a lot like that of *inglés).*
*El sofá está **enfrente de** la mesa.*   The sofa is in front of the table.

HOT TIPS!

- Try these with action words like ***vive*** (lives) or ***trabaja*** (works).

  adentro; dentro de
  al lado de
  afuera; fuera de
  enfrente de
  encima de
  en
  debajo de
  detrás de
  arriba
  abajo

- Create ways to practice these words with commands.

- *Acerca de* means "about" and shouldn't be confused with *cerca de* (near).

- *Reminder:* ***estar*** tells "where"

The Wimpy Wonder Words

Cosas grandes often come in small packages. In Spanish, there are a handful of tiny words which can be heard often because of their extreme importance. (You have to listen closely!)

de (from, of)...
a (to)...
para (for)...

mí. (me)
usted. (you)
él. (him)
ella. (her)
ellos. (them)
ustedes. (you guys)
nosotros. (us)

_____ (name of person, place, or thing)

And watch for these "Wee wonders!"

sin   without
con   with; check the changes:
- **con**migo   with me
- **con**sigo   with you, him, her, them
- **con**tigo   with you (between friends, family)

See how the ¿quién? words change slightly when followed by "where" words!

HOT TIP!

Blend 'em together! *a* and *de* always mesh with *el:*
del Soy **del** pueblo. I'm **from** town.
al   Voy **al** parque. I'm going **to** the park.

Get It Together —Part II

No more fooling around. It's time for the amateurs to step aside. This stuff is for the "Pros" only!

Now that action words have been introduced, let's see what they look like when we "combine" them with all the other stuff. The key is to continue building strings of words—much like we do in English—but without fear of making mistakes!

Here's a simple formula:

La persona + La acción + Lugar + Tiempo = ¡Mucho español!
 person   action   place   time

Roberto está trabajando en la tienda ahorita.
 Robert   is   working   in the store   right now.

To elaborate, add **descripción** and *detail!*

Mi amigo Roberto está trabajando en la tienda nueva hoy con María.
My friend Robert is working at the new store today with Maria.

Mis amigos americanos, Bob y Ed, no están trabajando mucho en la tienda nueva, porque ellos tienen clases todos los días.
My American friends, Bob and Ed, aren't working a lot at the new store, because they have classes every day.

Try mixing the order of your phrases.

Tengo el brazo quebrado, y el sábado no puedo jugar en el parque con las otras muchachas.
I have a broken arm, and I can't play at the park with the other girls on Saturday.

Or, how about forming a *pregunta?*

¿Su hermana va a la tienda, y va a comprar la comida para la cena y los dulces para los niños?
Is your sister going to the store and is she going to buy food for dinner and candy for the kids?

HOT TIPS!

- A "change" in the word order does not usually affect the meaning of the message!
- When you need to stop and "collect your thoughts," why not mutter a pause word, such as *¡Momento!*

There isn't a thing you can't talk about!

Un elefante gordo estaba bañandose en el río ayer y estaba comiendo las plantas debajo del agua.
A fat elephant was bathing in the river yesterday and was eating the plants under the water.

When you get *bueno* at combining your Spanish words, the *el* and *la* Business, the Reversal Rule and the Once-and-for-all Rule will be applied without effort—automatically! Just remember, the more you "babble," the better you'll be!

Also, lengthen those commands! Check back on the *mundatos* and "add on" a few *palabras*:

¡Hable!   Speak!
¡Hable con María   Speak with Mary!
...add some more:
¡Hable con María en la oficina!   Speak with Mary in the office!

And don't forget to combine two or more commands with the little linkers—*de, a, para, sin,* and *con:*
*¡**Vaya** a la escuela y **hable** con María en la oficina!*
Go to the school and **speak** with Mary in the office.

NOTE
Please say *Por favor.*

RSVP

As your strings of *palabras* get longer you'll need techniques to help you over any minor hurdles that may impede communication. Instead of walking away from a good conversation, try the RSVP (*R*epeat, *S*lur, *V*isualize, *P*ause) method of keeping things going. RSVP works, so master it *ló mas pronto posible* (as soon as possible).

Repeat it!

- Repeating what you hear is still one of the best ways to acquire language while conversing. Hearing and saying (instead of doing nothing at all) new words more than once, make comprehension and speech that much easier. *¿Comprende? ¡Comprende!*

Slur it!

- As ridiculous as it may seem, while you're learning Spanish, one very safe way to stay in a conversation is to slur and mumble those words, or parts of words, that you're not sure of. Using English, Spanglish, and even "creating" your own Spanish words are also very effective ways to reduce your "drop-out" rate.

Visualize it!

- When listening or speaking, just *picture* the unfamiliar words in their written form! Since Spanish is always pronounced exactly like it is spelled, comprehension is easy. Try it and you'll SEE!

And are you still using the other "Visualization" technique? Keep playing those *word-picture* association games. Here are some of my favorites:
libro (book)   looks like *library*
cuartos (rooms)   looks like *quarters*

P-a-u-s-e it!

- For those moments of silence when you're desperately trying to recall words and form a response, try muttering these life savers!

...*a ver*...	Let's see...	...*este*...	Uh...
...*o sea*...	What I mean is...	...*bueno*...	OK...
...*es decir*...	That is to say...	...*pues*...	Well...

HOT TIP!
- Spanish mutterings are like those in English, so put two or three *in a row!* Well...let's see...OK!

Not Much More to *Fluency!*

9

CHAPTER *NUEVE*

¡Bienvenidos!
(Welcome...to the Majors!)

¿Quiere jugar? ("Wanna Play?")

Americans love sports and recreation. And so do many Spanish speakers worldwide. For the Latin American, soccer is the king of sports. (They call it *fútbol.*) *El béisbol* is popular as well; in fact, if you need "listening practice," many ball games are broadcasted on the radio in both English and Spanish. As for individual hobbies (*pasatiempos*) in Latin America, they vary from person to person, just as they do in the United States. So, which of the following Spanish words might be helpful to you in *your* spare time?

Keep in mind, many sound like *inglés!*

el básquetbol   basketball
el béisbol   baseball
el boliche   bowling
el boxeo   boxing
el fútbol   soccer
el fútbol americano   football
el tenis   tennis
el vólibol   volleyball

el hockey; el surf; el golf
Guess their meaning!

And here are some action words in the games category:
el correr   running
el esquiar   skiing
el montar a caballo   horseback riding
el navegar   sailing
el patinar   skating
el pescar   fishing

CHOOSE 'N USE!

- *¿Le gusta...o...?*   Do you like...(baseball, etc.) or...(football, etc.)?
- *No sé mucho de...*   I don't know much about...(fishing, checkers, etc.).
- *...es excelente para su salud.*   ...(Tennis, running, etc.) is great for your health.
- *Necesitamos...*   We need the...(net, ball, etc.).

How about these "winners"!
¿Juega Ud. tenis?   Do you play tennis? *¿Tantos?*   What's the score?
¿Quién ganó?   Who won?   *¿Quién perdió?*   Who lost?

el atleta athlete
el campo field
la cancha court
el entrenador coach
el equipo team
el estadio stadium
el gimnasio gymnasium

el juego game
el partido match
la pelota or *la bola* ball
la práctica practice
la raqueta racket
la red net
el uniforme uniform

*Mi **pasatiempo** favorito*   (My favorite **hobby**)
el ajedrez chess
el dibujar drawing
la fotografía photography
el juego de damas checkers
el leer reading
las monedas coins
el monopolio monopoly
los naipes or *las cartas*   cards
el poker poker
el rompecabezas puzzles
los sellos stamps
el tocar música playing music

Jugar con los juguetes (Play with Toys)

Besides *los juegos* (games), we all grow up *jugando con* (playing with) toys. Kids of all ages will want to know the Spanish words for some of the common play *cosas!*

HOT TIP!

For a "toy" *object,* it's *tren de juguete* Toy train.

las canicas   marbles
las caricaturas   cartoons
los chistes   jokes
los colores   crayons
los cubos   blocks
los fuegos   fireworks
el globo   balloon
la magia   magic
la muñeca   doll
el papalote   kite
los patines   skates
la pelota   ball
el rompecabezas   puzzle
el trompo   top
los trucos   trucks

A theatrical "play" (*obra de teatro*) is not the same word! Yet, if *el drama* is your thing, maybe you can use these words below:

el ceño   frown
chistoso   funny
la comedia   comedy
la diversión   fun
las lágrimas   tears
la risa   laughter
la sonrisa   smile
la tragedia   tragedy

"Play", to make music, is a totally different action word in Spanish—instead of *jugar,* use **tocar.** Check out how *tocar* sounds when combined with these popular *instrumentos musicales* (musical instruments):

Toca...
You, He or She plays...

Notice how many words look like *inglés!*

> *el piano* piano
> *el violín* violin
> *la guitarra* guitar
> *el saxofón* or *el saxófono*   saxophone
> *la trompeta* trumpet
> *el tambor* drum
> *el clarinete* clarinet

CHOOSE 'N USE!
- *Mi hijo quiere...*   My kid wants...(a guitar, etc.).
- *Tengo...y...*   I have...(a piano, etc.) and...(a violin, etc.).
- *¿Dónde puedo comprar...?*   Where can I buy...(a clarinet, etc.)?

Travel Treats!

We've already covered a few helpful areas for the traveler; such as transportation, shopping, and restaurant talk. The following collection of words, however, includes "the sweetest" of Spanish *palabras* and *frases*, which will assist not only the experienced *turista*, but the occasional vacationer as well. Let's begin with the "life-savers":

¿A qué distancia?   How far?
¿Cuál autobús?   Which bus?
¿Cuál calle?   Which street?
¿Cuánto tiempo?   How much time?
¿Está incluída(o)?   Is it included?
¿Está listo(a)?   Is it ready?
¿Está ocupada(o)?   Is it taken?
¿Hay agua potable?   Is there drinking water?
¿Puede ayudarme?   Can you help me?
¿Puede recomendar uno?   Can you recommend one?
¿Puedo pagar con esto?   Can I pay with this?
¿Puede repararlo?   Can you fix it?

And don't leave home, without...

Dónde está...?
Where's...?

<table>
<tr><td>la aduana   customs</td><td>el hotel   the hotel</td></tr>
<tr><td>el aeropuerto   the airport</td><td>el mapa   the map</td></tr>
<tr><td>la alberca   the pool</td><td>la parada del autobús   the bus stop</td></tr>
<tr><td>el banco   the bank</td><td>el restaurante   the restaurant</td></tr>
<tr><td>el camino a...   the road to...</td><td>el semáforo   signal light</td></tr>
<tr><td>el centro   downtown</td><td>la señal   road sign</td></tr>
<tr><td>el correo   the post office</td><td>el teléfono   the phone</td></tr>
<tr><td>la estación   the station</td><td>la tienda   the store</td></tr>
<tr><td>el hospital   the hospital</td><td>el tráfico   traffic</td></tr>
</table>

NOTE

Use your time-telling skills!
- *¿Qué hora es?*   What time is it?
- *¿A qué hora?*   At what time?

Unas personas necesarias
la criada   maid
el dueño   owner
el botones   bellboy
el conserje   concierge
el gerente   manager

Here's a mixed bag of "Good 'n Plenty":

Quiero (I want)**...**
Necesito (I need)**...**
Quisiera (I'd like)**...**

hacer reservaciones (to make reservations),
cargarlo (to charge it),
pagarlo (to pay it),
cambiarlo (to exchange it),
hacer una llamada (to make a call),
ordenar (to order),
un boleto (a ticket),
la llave (the key),
un taxi (a taxi),
más toallas (more towels),
una habitación (a room),
más hielo (more ice),
una bebida (a drink),
la cuenta (the bill),
un corte de pelo (a haircut)

...por favor!

El carro (The car)

el aceite oil
el agua water
la batería battery
la gasolina gas
los litros de normal liters of regular
el motor engine
la llanta desinflada flat tire
¡Llénelo! Fill it up!

¡La pesca! (Fishing)

el anzuelo hook
la bahía bay
el barco boat
la caña rod
el carrete reel
el cordel line

el guía guide
la isla island
lanzar to cast
la marea tide
el nudo knot
las olas waves

el pescado fish
el pescador fisherman
pescar to fish
la punta point
la red net
las rocas rocks

¡Márquelo y Suéltelo! **Tag** it and **release** it!

Now, sample these "suckers"!

el alfiler pin
la bolsa bag
la botella bottle
la caja box
la carta letter
la cerradura lock
el champú shampoo
los cigarillos cigarettes
el desodorante deodorant
el enjuague conditioner
los fósforos matches
el hilo thread
el jabón soap

la lata can
la medicina medicine
las navajas razors
el papel higiénico toilet paper
el periódico newspaper
la propina tip
el recado message
la revista magazine
el rollo de la película roll of film
el sello stamp
el sobre envelope
la tarjeta postal postcard

El dinero

($)

Find out the names for the currency and its rate of exchange before you travel anywhere. "Practice" pronouncing the words and phrases you'll need for a few days before you leave!

Survival Signs

In traveling, the key to success is *awareness.* So keep your *ojos* open for these common letreros (signs) and you won't be "lost."

ABIERTO Open	*EMPUJE* Push
ADUANA Customs	*ENTRADA* Entrance
ALTO Stop	*ESTACIONAMIENTO* Parking
CEDA EL PASO Yield	*GLORIETA* Traffic Circle
CERRADO Closed	*NO FUMAR* No Smoking
CIRCULACIÓN One Way	*NO REBASE* No Passing
CRUZ ROJA Red Cross	*SALIDA* Exit
DESCOMPUESTO Out of Order	*SANITARIOS* Restrooms
DESPACIO Slow	*SE ALQUILA* For Rent
DESVIACIÓN Detour	*SE VENDE* For Sale
EMERGENCIA Emergency	*JALE* Pull

Las medidas (Measurements)
(Study your metrics!)
el litro liter
el metro meter
el kilómetro $= \, ^5/_8$ mile
el kilogramo $=$ 2.2 lbs.
And ask folks about any *abbreviations* you see!

CHOOSE 'N USE!

- *Primero vamos a buscar...*   First let's look for the...(passport, bellhop, etc.).
- *¿Qué significa...?*   What does...(customs, for rent, etc.) mean?
- *Présteme...*   Lend me the...(camera, key, etc.).

What's in a *nombre?*

It's amazing how much influence Spanish has had over the years in many parts of the United States. Yet, we seldom stop to ponder the meaning of names of many of our cities, states, and landmarks. Some of them may surprise you.

Alamo (Poplar tree)
Amarillo (Yellow)
Colorado (Red)
El Paso (The pass)
Florida (Flowery)
Las Vegas (The plains)
Los Angeles (The angels)
Montana (Mountain)

Nevada (Snowfall)
Rio Grande (Large river)
Sacramento (Sacrament)
San Antonio (Saint Anthony)
San Diego (Saint James)
San Francisco (Saint Francis)
Santa Fe (Holy Faith)
Sierras (Mountain range)

Southwestern Specials

There's one part of the United States that's got *español* literally *everywhere!* Here are words that can be *seen* or *heard* throughout the Southwest:

agua (water)
arroyo (creek)
costa (coast)
loma (hill)
mar (sea)
mira (look)
misión (mission)
monte (mountain)

palo (stick, stump)
playa (beach)
puerto (port)
real (royal)
río (river)
santa or *san* (saint)
valle (valley)
vista (view)

- *avenida* (Avenue)
- *calle* (Street)

- *camino* (Road)
- *del* (of the)

And how about ***los nombres de personas!*** Obviously, those listed here are only the most prevalent. Yours may or may not have an equivalent. (*Ask around*!)

Male Names

Al *(Alfredo)*
Bob *(Roberto)*
Charlie *(Carlos)*
Ed *(Eduardo)*
Frank *(Francisco)*
George *(Jorge)*
Jim *(Jaime)*
Joe *(José)*
John *(Juan)*
Mark *(Marcos)*
Mike *(Miguel)*
Peter *(Pedro)*
Rick *(Ricardo)*
Steve *(Estéban)*
Tom *(Tomás)*
William *(Guillermo)*

Female Names

Alice *(Alicia)*
Ann *(Ana)*
Barb *(Bárbara)*
Carol *(Carolina)*
Debbie *(Débora)*
Helen *(Elena)*
Jane *(Juanita)*
Kathy *(Catalina)*
Liz *(Isabel)*
Lynn *(Lina)*
Marge *(Margarita)*
Martha *(Marta)*
Mary *(María)*
Nancy *(Anita)*
Sally *(Sara)*
Susan *(Susana)*

HOT TIPS!

- Some names are written the same in both languages: David, Samuel, Daniel, Gloria, Linda, Virginia.
- Some have "nicknames": *Francisco "Nacho"* *Guillermo "Memo"* *José "Pepe"*
- And add ***-ito*** for endearment. *Juan "Juan**ito**"*

That's *Amor*

This guidebook would be incomplete without the presentation of the most significant Spanish "love lines." Romance is only a few *palabras* away.

Soy...	*casad**o(a)***	married
I'm...	*solter**o(a)***	single
	*divorciad**o(a)***	divorced
	*viud**o(a)***	widowed

"Power Lines"

Estoy enamorado(a).   I'm in love.
Es una promesa.   It's a promise.
¿Le gustó(a)? Did you enjoy it?
Me divertí mucho(a).   I had a nice time.
¿Puedo verle más tarde?   Can I see you later?
¿Quieres casarte conmigo?   Will you marry me?
¿Quisiera...   Would you like to...
   bailar?   to dance?
   dar un paseo?   take a walk?
   platicar?   chat?
   salir?   leave?
Te quiero.   I love you.

¿Cómo es?   (What's he, or she, like?)

Es…
He's or She's…

agradable pleasant
amistoso(a) friendly
apasionado(a) passionate
aplicado(a) studious
bonita pretty
celoso(a) jealous
cruel mean
educado(a) well-mannered
fiel faithful
guapo(a) handsome

honesto(a) honest
responsable responsible
romántico(a) romantic
simpático(a) nice
sincero(a) sincere
tímido(a) shy

- *besos.* kisses XXXX.
- *abrazos.* hugs OOOO.

Nice Things to Say

Girl to boy/Boy to girl:

chulo/a cute
mi amor my love
mi corazón sweetheart
mi dulce my sweet
mi tesoro/a my treasure
mi vida love of my life
querido/a darling
precioso/a precious

Boy to girl only:

bella beautiful
hermosa lovely
linda very pretty
mi reina my queen

- Embrace these words!

  los amantes   the lovers
  el aniversario anniversary
  la boda wedding
  el cine movie
  el concierto concert
  la fiesta party
  el matrimonio marriage
  los novios the engaged
  la pareja the couple

- A "date" is *una cita.*

HOT TIP!

Lovers and friends use the word *tú* for "you" instead of *usted. (Tú) Eres* means "you are"!

CHOOSE 'N USE!
- *¡Él es tan…!* He is so…(cute, romantic, etc.).
- *¡Sí! Pero es muy…también.* Yes, but he's very…(shy, cruel, etc.) also.
- *Mi…, te quiero tanto.* My…(darling, love, etc.), I love you so much.
- *Nos conocimos en….* We met at a…(wedding, concert, etc.).

La religión, la política, y la filosofía

You can guess what *la religión, la política,* and *la filosofía* mean. And although it's better to avoid such controversial topics in any language, there's a chance they may pop up in beginning *conversación.* So if you're interested in the *argumento inevitable,* arm yourself with these fiery fundamental words:

la cárcel	jail	*la ley*	law
el castigo	punishment	*la mayoría*	majority
el comunismo	communism	*las mentiras*	lies
la corte	courtroom	*la minoría*	minority
el crimen	crime	*el partido*	political party
la culpa	blame	*el pleito*	lawsuit
la democracia	democracy	*el público*	public
los derechos	rights	*el racismo*	racism
el gobierno	government	*la verdad*	truth
la justicia	justice	*el voto*	vote

El mundo (The world)

las armas	weapons	*las pandillas*	gangs
el cáncer	cancer	*la paz*	peace
la contaminación	pollution	*la pobreza*	poverty
las drogas	drugs	*el respeto*	respect
la enfermedad	sickness	*el sexo*	sex
la esperanza	hope	*el SIDA*	AIDS
el estrés	stress	*los terroristas*	terrorists
la guerra	war	*la violencia*	violence
la huelga	strike		

- *amar*   to love
- *odiar*   to hate

Yo creo... ("I believe...")

el ángel	angel	*la Virgen*	the Virgin
la Biblia	Bible	*el alma*	soul
los católicos	Catholics	*el cielo*	heaven
los cristianos	Christians	*el fantasma*	ghost
el diablo	devil	*la fé*	faith
Diós	God	*el funeral*	funeral
el Espíritu Santo	Holy Spirit	*el infierno*	hell
Jesucristo	Jesus Christ	*el milagro*	miracle
los judíos	Jews	*la muerte*	death
los mormones	Mormons	*el muerto*	dead
los musulmanes	Moslems	*la vida*	life
los santos	saints		

- *¿Qué piensa de...?*   What do you think of...?
- *En mi opinión...*   In my opinion...
- *Según...*   According to...

Whenever heavy topics are discussed, play it safe! Make *comentarios* with those "one-a-day" one-liners!

La cultura hispánica

Language and culture are inseparable. Therefore, it's imperative that we take time to look closely at the people who speak Spanish. Who are they? Where do they come from? What are their values, traditions, and life styles? Only through understanding one's *cultura* can true communication take place. Chatting is fine, but knowing where the speaker is "coming from" makes all the difference. So do a little research. Read up on Puerto Rican customs, Cuban society, or Mexican history. Learn by asking. Find out about family relationships, foods, and traditional holidays. And keep an open mind. Conversations always become more meaningful when there is mutual respect and consideration.

There's no way we can generalize and stereotype Spanish speakers. Folks from Cuba, Puerto Rico, and Mexico are not *all alike*. Sure, they share the same language, but each nation's heritage, diet, and everyday conversations differ in several ways. First, let's check out a few *diferencias*. These are considered popular among folks from Cuba, Puerto Rico, and Mexico:

Cuba

¡No chive!   Don't bother me!
¿Oigo?   Hello? (on phone)
¡Hola mi socio!   Hi, pal!
¡Concho!   Darn!
¡Oye chico, no seas patán!   Hey, don't be a jerk!
Zanjar un asunto.   To solve a problem.

Puerto Rico

¡Oye, tocayo!   Hey, buddy!
¡Oye mi pana!   Hi, pal!
Na más.   Nothin' else.
¡Tranca la boca!   Shut up!
Ser la medio guayaba de...   To
  be ...'s wife.
Saltar el charco.   Fly to New York.

Notice *how* they talk!

Mexico

¿Mande?   How's that?
¡Pásele!   Go ahead!
¿Bueno?   Hello? (on phone)
¡Ay chihuahua!   Oh, my gosh!
¡Andele!   Hurry up!
¿Qué traes?   What's new?
Güero.   Blond.
Hue.   Buddy.

Unas palabras básicas…

Cuba

blumers underwear
espejuelos glasses
fregar platos wash dishes
gomas tires
gua-gua bus
haragán lazy
jimagua twin
maní peanuts
mima mom
mi viejo my friend
pipo dad
servicio toilet
timón steering wheel

Mexico

charreadas rodeos
guacamole avocado sauce
guajolote turkey
huaraches sandals
maíz corn
mariaches musicians
pisto money
rancheras ranch songs
sarape blanket
tardeadas afternoon parties
vaqueros cowboys

Puerto Rico

batey front yard
bodega grocery store
chino orange
caucho sofa
frisa blanket
guineo banana
melón watermelon
negrito loved one
papito daddy
pelea del gallo cockfight
sombrilla umbrella
traje dress

Las comidas tradicionales (Traditional Foods)

Here are a few very popular dishes served throughout Mexico, Cuba, and Puerto Rico. *I recommend them all!*

Mexican Food
(Comida mexicana)

albóndigas (meat-ball soup)

barbacoa (BBQ lamb)

birria (shredded goat meat)

bolillos (rolls)

buñuelos (deep fried donuts)

burrito (wrapped and filled flour tortilla)

caldo (soup)

carne asada (grilled beef strips)

carnitas (roast pork)

chile relleno (stuffed pepper)

enchiladas (usually cheese)

flan (vanilla pudding)

flautas (deep fried taco)

frijoles (beans, of course)

huevos rancheros (eggs with salsa)

lengua (cow's tongue)

mariscos (sea food)

menudo (tripe soup)

mole (chicken, turkey, or pork in sauce)

nachos (chips and cheese)

nopales (diced cactus)

pan dulce (Mexican pastry)

pozole (soup with pork)

quesadilla (cheese on tortillas)

sope (small, pizzalike)

taco (soft, not hard)

tamal (wrapped in corn husk)

tortillas (corn or flour)

tostada (flat and fried)

HOT TIP!

Ask "how" certain foods are eaten, or "how" they are prepared.

Cuban Food *(Comida cubana)*

ajiaco (vegetable and meat soup)

arroz a la cubana (white rice and fried egg)

arroz congrí (rice with black beans)

arroz con leche (rice, milk, and sugar)

arroz con pollo (rice with chicken)

frijoles negros (black beans)

tostones (banana chips)

yuca con mojo (potatolike vegetable)

Puerto Rican Food
(Comida puertorriqueña)

arroz con gandules (exotic rice and bean dish)

arroz guisado (stew and rice)

arroz y habichuelas rojas (rice and kidney beans)

bacalao (pickled codfish)

mofongo (large fried green banana dish)

pasteles (musk-wrapped dish)

sofrito (spicy seasoning)

vianda (starchy vegetables)

10

CHAPTER *DIEZ*
Las últimas palabras
(Last Words)

Talk About Language

Eventually, during the Spanish learning experience you will be forced to communicate with the "language" words commonly found in textbooks. (Remember these from English class?)

el adverbio   adverb
el capítulo   chapter
la conjugación   conjugation
el diálogo   dialog
el ejemplo   example
el ejercicio   exercise
la escritura   the writing
la estructura   structure
el estudio   study
el exámen   test
la frase   sentence
la gramática   grammar
el hablar   speech
el idioma   language
la lección   lesson
la lectura   the reading
la manera or *el modo*
   the manner
la mayúscula   capital letter

el método   the method
la minúscula   lower case letter
la página   page
las palabras   words
la práctica   practice
la pregunta   question
el pronombre   pronoun
la pronunciación   pronunciation
el repaso   review
el símbolo   symbol
el significado   meaning
el sonido   sound
el sujeto   subject
el sustantivo/el nombre   noun
la tarea   homework
el tema   theme
el verbo   verb
el vocabulario   vocabulary
la voz   voice

Things *you* might say:

- *¡El estudio de la gramática no es muy importante!*   The study of grammar is not very important!
- *¡Necesito más práctica y repaso!*   I need more practice and review!
- *¡No me gustan los exámenes y las tareas!*   I don't like tests and homework!
- *¡Comprendo el significado del vocabalario!*   I understand the meaning of the vocabulary!

Práctica, práctica, práctica (Practice!)

Traditionally, foreign language "practice" involved completion of grammar exercises, dialog memorization, and hours of audiolingual drills in a language lab. *Good News!* Practice techniques have changed—and in my opinion, for the better. The following methods are currently being applied worldwide in the most successful programs. And they're all based on the latest discoveries in second-language research.*

Learning Vocabulario

- Use the **command** words! Combine them with names of things you'd like to know. Use real objects or pictures of items. Have a friend "order you" to touch or move whatever it is you're learning.

- **Interview** Spanish speakers! List items like *sports* or *foods* and ask individuals which ones they like or dislike. Use a question like *¿Le gusta a Ud....?* (Do you like...?) and check off their responses.

- Collect Spanish children's books, coloring books, or toys. Since you're a "child" in the language, it's important to have lots of **visual exposure** to new words. While reading, point to each picture and "name it" in *español.* (This is really fun to do with the kids!)

- Make an audio **tape.** Ask a native Spanish speaker to read aloud a list of words that you need to know. Tape different people, so you can hear all the different sounds. At first, don't bother with vocabulary you're not going to use every day. And offer to make an English tape in return!

- **Draw** pictures of items in special categories, and then **label** them. (The "unartistic," can cut out pictures from magazines!)

> **NOTE**
> Although it's not always feasible, these activities work better when learners are assisted by *native* Spanish speakers.

Comidas (Foods)

manzana   plátano   coco   melón

---

*Krashen, Stephen D. and Terrell, Tracy D. *The Natural Approach.* Hayward, California: The Alemany Press, 1983.

• **Be creative!** For example, practice descriptive words by drawing
either a strange-looking monster or your dream date!

muy gordo	*mucho dinero*
cuatro brazos	*muy bonita*
tres ojos	*muy inteligente*
orejas grandes	
_____	_____
_____	_____

HOT TIP!

*If you've got the
time,* cut out the
vocabulary pages in
this book and make
games like Bingo or
Concentration. (Fun
for the whole family!)

Learning Basic *Conversaciones*

The best advice I can offer to those wanting experience in basic Spanish chit-chat is: *Just do it!* However, to "practice" conversation on your own, here are two helpful suggestions.

- A fun game one can play with a new language is to "white-out" words from the funnies, and then make up "foreign" responses which relate to the pictures. Use *any* Spanish words you know. (Write it in or just *say it!*)

- On paper, create a dialog of your own—*one that you need* and will use often. With scissors, cut out each one-liner, phrase, and so on; then, mix them up. Practice putting the pieces in order so that it makes sense.

Bien, gracias. ¿Y usted?

Muchas gracias. Adiós.

José está en la oficina.

Bien. ¿Dónde está José?

Hola. ¿Cómo está?

Por nada. Hasta luego.

Learning *Acciones*

Unquestionably, the most natural way to acquire action words is by having someone command you "to do something." In acting out the command, you "pick up" on the action word used. On the other hand, with **"visuals,"** you can begin to "talk" about what's going on. And creating your own "visuals" is easy. All you need are some paper, a few old magazines, glue, and a pair of scissors. Use the models given below, or develop your own. Get friends and family involved. Let that imagination run wild! Let's begin with a "visual" that helps teach the *affirmative, negative,* and *question* forms. Try these with *comiendo* (eating).

With a chart, we can expand on the action words!

The visuals can be "read":

a.   *Yo **no** estoy comiendo manzanas.*
b.   *Ella está comiendo plátanos*
c.   *¿Ellos están comiendo naranjas?*

d.   *¡Nosotros _____ _____ _____ _____!*

And this picture-story is for the super-star who already knows a bunch of action words. Go box to box, and tell what's happening in each picture. (When you get really *bueno en español,* you'll be able to answer questions about the story, such as "What happened last night?" or "What happens every day?") You're not that far away.

Learning *"Grammar"*

As in all languages, in Spanish, grammar or "grammatical structure" is acquired "naturally" through trial and error. That's why a child's sentences always sound "so cute." It takes years of mistakes (and hours of classroom instruction) before anyone is able to respond consistently—using "proper grammar." Fortunately, for second-language learners there is a shortcut. Recent studies indicate that reading is one way to "fast and painless" language acquisition. Thus, by reading Spanish, learners can "pick up" basic rules of *la gramática española.* It seems that when GRINGOS read simple, interesting Spanish material regularly, their spoken Spanish improves—and their grammar usage becomes *correcto* most of the time!

The following is a brief story filled with the information introduced in Chapters 3 to 8. Before you read it, go back and skim the chapters. Then, read through the story. Next, check the chapters again to confirm comprehension.

> **NOTE**
> Comic books work very well for this activity. Or, for the more industrious, cut out and paste magazine photos of people in action to light cardboard or construction paper. They make super flash cards!

- Collect varied Span-
ish reading materials!
In addition to *books,
newspapers,* and
magazines—gather
inserts, labels, bro-
chures, flyers, forms,
posters, etc. (*Words
with pictures* are
best.)
- *Librerías* (book-
stores), *bibliotecas*
(libraries), and
papelerías (station-
ery stores), *quioscos*
(newsstands) sell or
loan out literature for
all reading levels.
(Browsing in these
places is nice—*you
don't have to say a
word!*)
- Avoid stopping to
"study" words and
sentences! Calmly
skim over what you
don't understand and
try to focus on the
main idea of each
paragraph.
- At home, practice
reading *aloud.* Tape
yourself, play it back,
and then note any
obvious "sound-
making" problems.
(For best results,
"read along" with
native speakers!)
- Memorizing jokes,
tongue-twisters,
rhymes, and folk
songs is a fantastic
way to gain confi-
dence while learning
language skills.

Una historia   (A Story)

Yo soy Roberto. Ahora estoy muy bien. Tengo 28 años y no tengo muchos problemas. Estoy trabajando para una compañía grande en los Estados Unidos con muchos de mis amigos. Me gusta mi trabajo. Me gusta mi familia, también. Todos son de México. En mi casa están mi esposa, mis hijos, mi madre y mi abuelo. La casa es grande. Tiene cuatro recámaras, tres baños, una cocina grande y la sala. Pero no hay un garaje. Es un problema porque tengo un carro nuevo. Es un Toyota blanco.

Mi esposa y mi madre están trabajando ahora en un restaurante. Están muy contentas allí. Mis hijos están estudiando en las escuelas públicas. Son muy inteligentes. Están estudiando el inglés. Mi abuelo no está trabajando porque tiene problemas con su espalda.

El lunes no voy a trabajar. Estoy preparando todo para un viaje a México. Cada diciembre toda la familia tiene una fiesta grande en nuestro pueblo. El pueblo está en las montañas, y es necesario comprar mucha comida y ropa especial. Por ahora estoy traba-jando horas extra para pagar por el viaje.

Ahora estoy trabajando "overtime."

The popular close and open-ended techniques are used in stories to teach both grammar and vocabulary. Certain words are deleted, and readers insert any appropriate vocabulary. So "exchange" the under-lined words for others! (the same could also be done with the action words!) Personal tales involving daily activities appear to work best.

Unas preguntas para Ud. (Some Questions for You)

Here are 22 common *preguntas* you **should** now be able to answer. *(Por favor,* be brief!)

¿Cómo está usted?
¿Cómo se llama usted?
¿Cuál es su número de teléfono?
¿Quién es el presidente de los E.E.U.U.?
¿De quién es este libro?
¿Le gusta a usted la música clásica?
¿Qué hora es?
¿Qué día es hoy?
¿Qué tiempo hace?
¿Cuáles son tres partes del cuerpo?
¿Cuántas hermanas tiene usted?
¿Hay un doctor en su familia?
¿Dónde trabaja usted?
¿Es muy bonita la Mona Lisa?
¿Dónde está su cama?
¿Es usted de los Estados Unidos?
¿Tiene usted hambre?
¿Cuántos años tiene usted?
¿Qué está haciendo usted?
¿Qué están haciendo los miembros de su familia?
¿Cuándo habla usted el español?
¿Qué está detrás de usted?

The Answers?
...Write 'em
or
Just say 'em!
and
sorry, but you'll have to check 'em yourself!

Following are ten preguntas you **might** be able to answer!
¿Sabe usted mucho español?
¿A dónde va usted mañana?
¿Se lava usted las manos todos los días?
¿Quién fue el primer presidente de los Estados Unidos?
¿Dónde estaba usted anoche?
¿Quiere usted ir a Disneylandia?
¿Tiene usted miedo de los gatos negros?
¿Puede usted jugar las canicas?
¿De dónde es usted?
¿Habla usted con la aduana mucho?

Before I Say *Adiós*...

Without a doubt, this was the most difficult part of the entire guidebook to write. What more can I say? Everything you really need to get started in Spanish has already been introduced. (I know, because I once was in your *zapatos*.) Nevertheless, to make it all really work, I decided to summarize my thoughts in a series of closing remarks, personal comments and easy-to-follow suggestions which, when considered, lead gringo learners to immediate success in Spanish. *Por favor*, take heed.

Three Big Steps to
Comunicación

NEXT:

Spanish for Gringos 2... and beyond!

Third: You need to use the "*-ndo's*"

Second: You've got to feel good about the *"Big Five"*

First: You've got to know the *"Secrets to Soundmaking"*

Five Things to Always Keep In Mind

1 *Pronunciation* and *grammar* don't really matter!
2 You don't have to speak until you feel like doing it!
3 Feeling comfortable around non-English speakers makes a difference!
4 You can't make any excuses for not learning!
5 Language learning takes place when you *relax* and have fun!

The Secrets to Success (All of these have already been mentioned. They are all *muy, muy importante!*)

- Try to be sensitive to and aware of cultural differences.
- Get in the habit of using Spanish *regularly.*
- Constantly memorize vocabulary through "word-picture" association.
- Experiment, take chances, and guess when you are unsure!
- Follow the practice tips and activities mentioned throughout *Spanish for Gringos.*
- *Add your own* ideas on how to practice and improve! This guide-book only establishes a base for your entire Spanish learning experience. Ask around, listen, and "build" from here.

Some *más* Advice:

- Try relaxation techniques before you "go for it." Stress-relief literature is available everywhere.
- Don't "stop in the middle" to translate! Whenever you're listening, concentrate on the topic first, so that you have some idea of what's going on.
- Aggressive, outgoing, fun-loving Gringos usually learn Spanish faster than others. A childlike attitude also seems to help!
- When you are in an embarrassing situation, stuck, confused, or at a loss for Spanish words, rely on these for help: *Lo siento.* (I'm sorry.) *No recuerdo la palabra.* (I don't remember the word.) *Estoy estudiando español.* (I'm studying Spanish.)

NOTE

Do not memorize these rules! Simply be aware of the problems facing the beginner! Remember that "being close" is good enough. Besides, *all* of this stuff is picked up *muy rápido* once you actually get started.

- Please say *por favor.* In Spanish, you'll go far if you are courteous. The more respectful you are, the more Spanish you'll learn. So practice "polite" things to say. And as always—be sincere.
- Be patient! I know what the word "busy" means—but life's too short to pass up those rare opportunities to practice talking Spanish with someone. Trust me—take the extra moments *now* or later you'll regret not doing so.
- Some words mean *two* or *more* things in Spanish. Find out the appropriate use for each meaning. Dictionaries often help—but be careful! (It's always better to go *straight to the source.)*
- Spanish speakers of different countries don't all agree! It's not uncommon for them to "clash" over meanings of words, customs, or historical events. That's why it's important to be aware of the differences between Hispanic dialects. Try to be good at guessing where folks are from!

The Gringo Nightmares (*Problemas* we all seem to have!)

- **The Secrets to Soundmaking**   Even though pronunciation doesn't need to be practiced, becoming familiar with the "*Big Five* and the *Others*" will definitely make understanding and speaking a whole lot easier. (In particular, watch out for the *e, a,* and *"i"*!) Remember, in Spanish you *always pronounce the letters the same. There are no exceptions!*
- **The *EL* and *LA* Business**   Again, although it won't effect communication much, practice putting *la* in front of objects ending with *a*, and *el* before those ending with *o*. (You'll just have to remember which one goes with words *not* ending in *o* or *a*.)
- **The Reversal Rule**   When describing things, giving the date, or telling "whose," *think backward!* In these instances, the Spanish word order is "reversed."
- **The Once-and-for-All Rule**   Another pattern that should be mentioned is the way in which strings of words have to "agree" in Spanish. "Agreement" is best understood by observing some examples. Notice how the words "agree" with each other:

Los libros buenos   The good books
La muchacha bonita   The pretty girl
Muchas casas negras y blancas   Lots of black and white houses

¡Mini-problemas!

Here are a handful of **palabras** that always seem to bother the GRINGO learner. Pay close attention—they're "sneaky":

poquito	a little bit	*de nada*	you're welcome
pequeño	small in size	*nada*	nothing
muy	very	*grande*	big
mucho	a lot	*largo*	long
número	number	*bueno*	good
nombre	name	*bien*	well
que	that	*jueves*	Thursday
qué	what	*huevos*	eggs
dólar	dollar	*hombre*	man
dolor	pain	*hambre*	hunger
sí	yes	*nuevo*	new
si	if	*nueve*	nine
esta	this one		
está	is		

Add some of your own!

_____ _____

_____ _____

It's entirely up to you how much *español* you'll eventually speak and understand. I hope that the easy-to-follow format has made your learning experience enjoyable—free of the stress and frustration of traditional programs. And probably by now you've discovered how the guidebook can be used to get best results. Use *Spanish for Gringos* any way you'd like! Set your own pace, take what you need, and reread only those pages that interest you. Some degree of language acquisition is guaranteed.

But this is really only the beginning. At the moment, you're merely crawling, standing, or staggering in the language. Trust me, fellow gringos, the best is yet to come.

Su amigo,

Bill

GUIDE TO SPANISH SOUNDMAKING
A Quick-check Reference to Basic Pronunciation

- Spanish words are pronounced exactly the way they are written.
- Knowing the BIG 5 (vowels) is the key to speaking and understanding Spanish.
- Poor pronunciation in Spanish does not seriously effect communication.
- Turn up the volume for the accented (´) parts of words. Spanish words without accents get more volume at the end, *unless* they end in A, E, I, O, U, N, or S. These get more volume on the *next to the last part*.
- Spanish words are "run-together" in short, choppy pieces, usually pronounced in the front part of the mouth, with little or no air being used to make the sounds.

APPENDIX
Vocabulary/*Vocabulario*

Most of the words introduced in *Spanish for Gringos* can be found in the glossary. Action word forms such as the "Command Words" and specialty vocabulary such as "Traditional Foods," are not part of the glossary. Such terms are listed by category in the Table of Contents.

El and *la* are given only when you might be uncertain which is required *(la acción, el ángel)*. Words that are the same or are both masculine and feminine are indicated by *el/la (el/la ayudante)*.

Note, too, that for convenience all verbs have been grouped under the "to" form on the English to Spanish side *(to allow, to answer, to arrange,* etc.).

You will also discover that some words may have multiple meanings or equivalents in the other language. However, the simple translations given here are general enough for basic conversational usage.

For more specific information, consult with a Spanish speaker, or refer to Barron's *Beginning Spanish Bilingual Dictionary*.

English — Spanish

a una, un
a little bit poco
a lot (*many*) muchos
a lot (*much*) mucho
a very little bit poquito
about acerca de
above encima
account cuenta
action la acción
actress la actriz
address la dirección
afterwards después
again otra vez
against contra
agency agencia
ahead adelante
AIDS el SIDA
air conditioning el aire acondicionado
airplane el avión
airport aeropuerto
all todo
almost casi
alone solo
along a lo largo de
already ya
also también
always siempre
American gringo, americano
and y
angel el ángel
angry enojado
animal el animal
anniversary aniversario
announcement anuncio
another otra, otro
ant hormiga
anxious ancioso
any cualquiera
anyone cualquiera persona
anywhere cualquiera parte
apartment apartamento
apple manzana
application la aplicación
appointment cita
April abril
apron el delantal
architect arquitecto
area code código de área
around alrededor de

ashtray cenicero
asleep dormido
asphalt asfalto
assistant el asistente
astronaut el astronauta
at en
at last por fin
athlete el atleta
attic el desván
August agosto
aunt tía
auto insurance seguro de auto
available disponible
avenue avenida
awhile rato
baby el bebé
backward al revés
bag bolsa
bakery panadería
bald calvo
ball bola, pelota
balloon globo
banana plátano
bank banco
bar (*drinking*) cantina
barber shop peluquería
bargain ganga
baseball el beisbol
basement sótano
basic básico
basketball el básquetbol
bathrobe bata de baño
bathroom baño
bathtub tina
battery batería
bay bahía
bear (*animal*) oso
beautiful bello
because porque
bed cama
bedroom recámara
bee abeja
beer cerveza
before antes
behind detrás
bellboy el botones
belt el cinturón
besides además
between entre

Bible Biblia
bicycle bicicleta
big grande
bill cuenta
billion el billón
bird pájaro
birth nacimiento
birthday el cumpleaños
bitter amargo
black negro
blackboard el pizarrón
blame culpa
blanket cobija
bleach el blanqueador
blender licuadora
block (*city*) cuadra
blond rubio
blouse blusa
blue azul
boat barco
book libro
bookcase librero
boot bota
border frontera
bored aburrido
boss el jefe
both ambos
bottle botella
bottom fondo
bowling el boliche
box (*container*) caja
boxing boxeo
boyfriend novio
bracelet el brazalete
branch rama
brave valiente
bread el pan
brick ladrillo
bride novia
bridge el puente
briefcase el maletín
briefly brevemente
bright brillante
bring traer
broken roto
brooch el broche
broom escoba
broth caldo
brother hermano
brother-in-law cuñado

brown pardo, café
brush cepillo
bucket el balde
buddy compañero
building edificio
bus el autobús
bus stop parada de autobús
bush arbusto
but pero
butter mantequilla
cabbage repollo
cabinet el gabinete
cake torta
calendar calendario
camel camello
camera cámara
campgrounds campamento
can lata
candy la dulce
cap gorra
capital (*letter*) mayúscula
car carro
car lot el lote de carro
card (*playing*) carta
cardboard el cartón
carpenter carpintero
carrot zanahoria
cartoon caricatura
cashier cajero
cat gato
Catholic católico
cement cemento
cemetery cementerio
Central America Centroamérica
certain cierto
chain cadena
chair silla
chalk tiza
change cambio
chapter capítulo
check el cheque
checkers juego de damas
cheese queso
chef cocinero
cherry cereza
chess el ajedrez
chicken pollo
child niña, niño
chimney chimenea

China China
Christian cristiano
Christmas la Navidad
church iglesia
cigarette cigarrillo
circus circo
clarinet el clarinete
clean limpio
clever listo
client el cliente
climate clima, tiempo
clock el reloj
closed cerrado
closet ropero
cloth tela
clothing ropa
cloud la nube
clown payaso
coach el entrenador
coast costa
cockroach cucaracha
coffee el café
coffee pot cafetera
coin moneda
cold frío
comb el peine
command mandato
communism comunismo
community la comunidad
computer computadora
concert concierto
conditioner (air) el acondicionador
conference conferencia
congratulations felicitaciones
contract contrato
conversation la conversación
cook cocinar
cooked cocido
cookie galleta
copier copiadora
corn el maíz
corner esquina
correct correcto
correctly correctamente
couch sofá
countryside campo
couple pareja, par
coupon el cupón
court (sport) cancha
court la corte
cousin primo
cow vaca
coward el cobarde
crab cangrejo
crazy loco
cream crema
credit card tarjeta de crédito
crime el crimen
cross la cruz
Cuba Cuba
cup taza
curtain cortina
customs aduana
cute chulo
daily diario
dance el baile
dangerous peligroso
dark oscuro
dark-haired moreno
darling querido
date fecha
daughter hija
daughter-in-law nuera
dawn madrugada

day el día
day before yesterday anteayer
dead muerto
death la muerte
deer venado
democracy democracia
dentist el dentista
deodorant el desodorante
description la descripción
desert desierto
desk escritorio
dessert el postre
detergent el detergente
detour la desviación
devil diablo
dialogue diálogo
diamond el diamante
dictionary diccionario
diet dieta
different diferente
difficult difícil
dining room el comedor
dirt tierra
dirty sucio
discount descuento
dish el traste
distance distancia
doctor médico
dog perro
doll muñeca
dollar el dólar
domestic doméstico
door puerta
doorbell el timbre
dot punto
doubt duda
down payment el enganche
downtown centro
downward abajo
drawer el cajón
dress vestido
dresser el tocador
drink bebida
driver's license licencia de chófer
drug droga
drum el tambor
dry seco
dryer secadora
duck pato
dumb tonto
during mientras
dusk el anochecer
dust polvo
each cada
early temprano
earring el arete
east este
easy fácil
easy chair el sillón
effectively efectivamente
egg huevo
eight ocho
eighteen diez y ocho
eighty ochenta
electric eléctrico
electricity la electricidad
elegant elegante
elephant el elefante
elevator el elevador
eleven once
emergency emergencia
employee empleado
empty vacío

end el fin
enemy enemigo
engine el motor
engineer ingeniero
England Inglaterra
English inglés
enough bastante
entrance entrada
envelope el sobre
every day todos los días
everybody todos, todo el mundo
everywhere por todas partes
example ejemplo
excellent excelente
exercise ejercicio
exit salida
expensive caro
experience experiencia
factory fábrica
faith la fé
faithful fiel
fall (season) otoño
family familia
famous famoso
fantastic fantástico
far lejos
farm finca
farmer campesino
fat gordo
father el padre
father-in-law suegro
fault falta, culpa
favorite favorito
fear miedo
feather pluma
February febrero
fence cerca
few pocos
fiancé novio
field campo
fifteen quince
fifty cincuenta
fight pleito
finally finalmente, por fin
fireman bombero
fireworks fuegos artificiales
first primer, primero
fish pez, el
fish (cooked) pescado
fisherman el pescador
five cinco
five hundred quinientos
flag bandera
flavor el sabor
floor piso
floor tile baldosa
flower la flor
fly (insect) mosca
fog neblina
following siguiente
food comida
for para, por
for rent se alquila
for sale se vende
forest el bosque
fork el tenedor
form forma
forward adelante
four cuatro
fourteen catorce
forty cuarenta
France Francia
fresh fresco
Friday viernes

fried frito
friend amigo
friendly amistos
from desde, de
frown ceño
frying pan la sartén
full lleno
fun la diversión
funny chistoso
furious furioso
furniture los muebles
furniture store mueblería
game juego
gang pandilla
garage el garaje
garden el jardín
gardener el jardinero
garlic ajo
gas station gasolinera
gate el portón
ghost el fantasma
giraffe jirafa
girlfriend novia
glass vidrio
glass (drinking) vaso
glove el guante
goat chivo
God Dios
gold oro
good bueno
good-bye adiós
government gobierno
grammar gramática
grandchild nieta, nieto
grandfather abuelo
grandmother abuela
grape uva
grapefruit toronja
grass pasto, hierba
gray gris
green verde
green bean judía verde
groom novio
guide el/la guía
guitar guitarra
gum el chicle
gymnasium gimnasio
haircut el corte de pelo
half la mitad, medio
hallway pasillo
ham el jamón
hamburger hamburguesa
hammer martillo
hand la mano
handkerchief pañuelo
handsome guapo
hanger gancho
hard (to touch) duro
hat sombrero
he él
health la salud
heart el corazón
heat el calor
heating la calefacción
heaven cielo
helicopter helicóptero
hell infierno
hello hola
helper el/la ayudante
her ella, su
here acá, aquí
hers suyo, suya
highway carretera
hill cerro
him él

hippopotamus hipopótamo
his su, suyo, suya
Hispanic hispánico, hispano
holy santo
homework tarea
honest honesto
honey la miel
hope esperanza
horse caballo
horseback riding montar a caballo
hose manguera
hospital el hospital
hot caliente
hot (*spicy*) picante
hot dog perro caliente
house casa
How many? ¿Cuántos?
How much? ¿Cuánto?
however sin embargo
hug abrazo
hundred cien
hundreds cientos
hunger el hambre
husband esposo
I yo
ice hielo
ice cream helado
if si
immediately inmediatamente
importance importancia
important importante
in en
in front of enfrente de
incorrect incorrecto
inexpensive barato
information la información
insect insecto
inside adentro
instrument instrumento
intelligent inteligente
interesting interesante
interview entrevista
introduction la introducción, la presentación
iron plancha
island isla
jacket chaqueta
jail la cárcel
January enero
Japan el Japón
jar frasco
jealous celoso
Jesus Christ Jesucristo
Jew judío
jewel joya
jewelry shop joyería
job trabajo
joke el chiste
juice jugo
July julio
June junio
jungle selva
just apenas
justice justicia
key la llave
kilogram (*2.2 pounds*) kilogramo
kilometer (*5/8 of a mile*) kilómetro
king el rey
kiss beso
kitchen cocina
kite papalote
knapsack mochila

knife cuchillo
knot nudo
ladder escalera
lady dama, señora
lake lago
lamp lámpara
language el idioma, lengua
large grande
last último
last night anoche
late tarde
later luego
Latin latino
laughter risa
laundromat lavandería
law la ley
lawyer abogado
lazy perezoso
leaf hoja
left (*direction*) izquierda
lemon el limón
lemonade limonada
less menos
lesson la lección
letter (*alphabet*) letra
letter (*mail*) carta
lettuce lechuga
library biblioteca
license plate placa
lie (*not true*) mentira
life vida
light la luz
light (*not dark*) claro
likewise igualmente
lion el león
list lista
liter litro
living room sala
lobster langosta
lock cerradura
long largo
lost perdido
love el amor
lovely hermoso
lover el amante
low bajo
lowercase (*letter*) minúscula
luck la suerte
magazine revista
magic magia
magnificent magnífico
maid criada
mail correo
majority mayoría
makeup el maquillaje
man el hombre
manager el gerente
manner manera
map mapa
marble (*toy*) canica
March marzo
marriage matrimonio
marvelous maravilloso
match fósforo
maximum máximo
May mayo
meal comida
mean cruel
meaning significado
meat la carne
meat market carnicería
mechanic mecánico
medicine medicina
medium mediano
meeting junta

member miembro
message recado
meter metro
method método
Mexico México
middle medio
midnight la medianoche
milk la leche
million el millón
millionaire millonario
mine mío
minority minoría
minute minuto
miracle milagro
mirror espejo
Miss señorita
mister el señor
modern moderno
moment momento
Monday lunes
money dinero
monkey mono
month el mes
mop el trapeador
more más
mother la madre
motorcycle motocicleta
mouse el ratón
movie el cine
Mr. sr. (*abr. for* señor)
Mrs. sra. (*abr. for* señora)
mud lodo
museum museo
music música
musician músico
mustard mostaza
my mi, mis
nail clavo
name el nombre
napkin servilleta
narrow estrecho
nation la nación
nationality la nacionalidad
nature naturaleza
near cerca
necessary necesario
necklace el collar
needle aguja
neighborhood barrio
neither tampoco
nervous nervioso
net la red
never nunca
nevertheless sin embargo
news las noticias
newspaper periódico
next próximo, siguiente
nice simpático
nightmare pesadilla
nine nueve
nine hundred novecientos
nineteen diez y nueve
ninety noventa
no one nadie
none ninguna, ninguno
noon el mediodía
North America Norteamérica
notations apuntes
note nota
notebook cuaderno
nothing nada
notice la notificación
November noviembre
nowadays ahora

nowhere por ningún lado
number número
nurse enfermera
nut (*food*) la nuez
obvious obvio
ocean océano
October octubre
of de
of the del
offer oferta
office oficina
oil el aceite
old viejo
older mayor
on en
once una vez
one uno
onion cebolla
only sólo
open abierto
operation la operación
opposite contrario
or o
orange (*fruit*) naranja
orange (*color*) anaranjado
our nuestra(s), nuestro(s)
out of order descompuesto
outlet el enchufe
outside afuera
outskirts las afueras
over sobre
over there allá
overcoat abrigo
owner dueño
page página
pain el dolor
paint pintura
painter el pintor
pair par, pareja
pajamas piyama
pants los pantalones
paper el papel
parents los padres
park el parque
parking estacionamiento
party fiesta
passionate apasionado
passport el pasaporte
past pasado
payment pago
pea el quisante
peace la paz
pearl perla
pen pluma
pencil el lápiz
people la gente
pepper pimienta
perfectly perfectamente
perfume el perfume
person persona
pharmacy farmacia
philosophy filosofía
phone number número de teléfono
photo la foto
photography fotografía
pie el pastel
pig puerco
pillow almohada
pin el alfiler
pitcher cántero
place el lugar, sitio
plant planta
plastic plástico
plate plato

playground patio de recreo
pleasant agradable
please por favor
pliers los alicates
plumber plomero
plumbing tubería
point punta
police policía
policy póliza
political party partido
politics política
pollution la contaminación
poor pobre
pork cerdo
possession la posesión
possible posible
post office (oficina de)
   correo
postcard tarjeta postal
pot olla
potato papa, patata
poverty pobreza
practice práctica
precious precioso
pregnant embarasada
presentation la presentación
president el presidente
pretty bonito
price precio
problem el problema
product producto
professional profesional
program programa
promise promesa
pronunciation la
   pronunciación
proud orgulloso
public público
punishment castigo
purple morado
purse bolsa
puzzle el rompecabezas
queen reina
question pregunta
quick rápido
quickly rápidamente
racket raqueta
rain lluvia
raincoat el impermeable
rake rastrillo
ranch rancho
rat rata
raw crudo
razor navaja
reading lectura
ready listo
reason la razón
receipt recibo
recipe receta
recreation recreo
red rojo
red-headed pelirrojo
refreshment refresco
refrigerator el refrigerador
relative el pariente
religion la religión
repair la reparación
reservation la reservación
respect respeto
restaurant el restaurante
restroom sanitario
review repaso
rhinoceros el rinoceronte
ribbon cinta
rice el arroz

rich rico
right (*direction*) derecha
right now ahora mismo
ring anillo
ripe maduro
river río
road camino
road sign la señal
rock roca
rocket el cohete
romantic romántico
room la habitación
rotten podrido
rough áspero
rubber goma
rug alfombra
sail navegar
saint santo
salad ensalada
sale venta
salesperson el vendedor,
   vendedora
salt la sal
salty salado
same mismo
same to you igualmente
sand arena
sangria sangría
Saturday sábado
sauce salsa
sausage salchicha
saw serrucho
saxophone saxófono, el
   saxofón
scarf bufanda
schedule horario
school escuela
scissors las tijeras
screw tornillo
screwdriver el destornillador
sea el/la mar
season la estación
second segundo
secretary secretario
seed semilla
seesaw el sube y baja
sentence la frase
September septiembre
seven siete
seven hundred setecientos
seventeen diez y siete
seventy setenta
several varios
sex sexo
shampoo el champú
she ella
sheep oveja
sheet (*bed*) sábana
sheet (*paper*) hoja
shirt camisa
shoe zapato
shoe store zapatería
short (*in height*) bajo
short (*in length*) corto
shorts los calzoncillos
shovel pala
shower ducha
shrimp el camarón
shy tímido
sickness la enfermedad
side lado
sidewalk acera
signal light semáforo
silver plata
sincere sincero

sincerely sinceramente
single soltero
sister hermana
sister-in-law cuñada
site sitio, el lugar
six seis
sixteen diez y seis
sixty sesenta
size tamaño
skates los patines
ski esquiar
skirt falda
skyscraper el rascacielos
slippers las pantúflas
slow lento
slowly despacio
small chico
smile sonrisa
smoke humo
smooth suave
snake víbora
snow la nieve
so tan
soap el jabón
soccer el fútbol
social security seguro social
socks los calcetines
soft blando
soldier soldado
some algún, algunos, algunas;
   uno(s), una(s)
someone alguien
sometimes a veces
somewhere por algún lugar
son hijo
son-in-law yerno
soon pronto
soul el alma
sound sonido
soup sopa
sour agrio
South America Sudamérica
Spain España
Spanish español
special especial
spend gastar
spider araña
spoon cuchara
sport el deporte
sports coat saco
spring primavera
stadium estadio
stain mancha
stairs las escaleras
stamp sello
station la estación
steak el bistec
step paso
stereo aparato estereofónico
stick palo
still aún
stone piedra
store tienda
stove estufa
strange extraño
strawberry fresa
street la calle
strike huelga
strong fuerte
structure estructura
student el estudiante
studious aplicado
study estudio
stupid estúpido
subway metro, (*abr. for*

   metropólitano)
suddenly de repente
sugar el/la azúcar
suit el traje
suitcase maleta
summer verano
Sunday domingo
sunset puesta del sol
supermarket supermercado
sure seguro
surname apellido
surprised sorprendido
sweater el suéter
sweatsuit el traje de
   entrenamiento
sweet dulce
sweethearts los novios
swimming pool piscina
swimsuit el traje de baño
symbol símbolo
T-shirt camiseta
table mesa
tablecloth el mantel
tall alto
tea el té
teacher maestro
team equipo
tear (*crying*) lágrima
telephone teléfono
television la televisión, el
   televisor
ten diez
tennis el tenis
terrible terrible
terrific terrífico
test el examen
thanks gracias
that que
that (*there*) esa, ese, eso
that (*one*) ésa, ése
the (*f*) la, las
the (*m*) el, los
their su, sus, suyos
theirs suyo
theme el tema
then entonces
there ahí
there is, there are hay
therefore por eso
these estos, estas
these ones éstos, éstas
they ellos, ellas
thief el ladrón
thin flaco
thing cosa
thirst la sed
thirteen trece
thirty treinta
this esto, esta, este
this one ésta, éste
those esos, esas
those (*over there*) aquéllos,
   aquéllas
thousand mil
thread hilo
three tres
throat garganta
Thursday jueves
ticket boleto
tide marea
tie corbata
tiger el tigre
time (*hour*) hora
time tiempo
tip propina

tire (*auto*) llanta
tired cansado
to a
to allow dejar
to answer contestar
to arrange arreglar
to arrive llegar
to attend asistir
to avoid evitar
to be ser
to be (*location and condition*) estar
to begin empezar
to bet apostar
to block obstruir
to break quebrar
to build construir
to carry llevar
to cast lanzar, tirar
to catch coger
to celebrate celebrar
to chat platicar
to check revisar
to climb subir
to close cerrar
to comb one's hair peinarse
to control controlar
to court someone pretender
to cry llorar
to cut cortar
to dance bailar
to develop desarrollar
to discuss discutir
to do hacer
to draw dibujar
to dream soñar
to drink beber, tomar
to enjoy oneself divertirse
to exit salir
to find encontrar
to finish terminar
to fish pescar
to fix reparar
to float flotar
to fly volar
to forget olvidar
to get dressed vestirse
to give dar
to guess adivinar
to happen suceder, pasar
to hate odiar
to have tener
to hit golpear, pegar
to join juntar
to kiss besar
to learn aprender
to leave salir
to leave behind dejar
to lend prestar
to lie down acostarse
to listen escuchar
to look for buscar

to lose perder
to love amar
to make hacer
to make a call hacer una llamada
to miss faltar
to order ordenar
to park estacionar
to pass pasar
to pay pagar
to pitch lanzar
to plant plantar
to play (*a game*) jugar
to play (*an instrument*) tocar
to pull jalar
to push empujar
to put poner
to quit renunciar
to raise oneself up levantarse
to read leer
to receive recibir
to rest descansar
to return volver
to ride (*on the back of an animal*) montar
to run correr
to save (*keep*) ahorrar
to say decir
to sell vender
to show mostrar
to sing cantar
to sit down sentarse
to skate patinar
to sleep dormir
to smoke fumar
to speak hablar
to stick pegar, adherir
to survive sobrevivir
to swim nadar
to take tomar
to take advantage aprovechar
to take away quitar
to throw tirar
to touch tocar
to translate traducir
to travel viajar
to trust confiar
to try probar
to type escribir a máquina
to visit visitar
to walk caminar
to wash lavar
to watch mirar
to weigh pesar
to wish desear
to work trabajar
to yell gritar
to yield ceder al
to the al
toaster tostador

today hoy
together juntos
toilet excusado
tomorrow mañana
tongue lengua, el idioma
too, also también
too much demasiado
tool herramienta
tourist el/la turista
towards hacia
towel toalla
town pueblo
traffic tráfico
train el tren
training entrenamiento
trash can el bote de basura
travel agency agencia de viajes
treasure tesoro
tree el árbol
truck el camión
truck driver camionero
truth la verdad
Tuesday martes
turkey pavo
twelve doce
twenty veinte
twin gemelo
two dos
typewriter máquina de escribir
umbrella el paraguas
underneath debajo
underwear ropa interior
United States Estados Unidos
university la universidad
until hasta
upward arriba
usually usualmente
vacation la vacación
vacuum cleaner la aspiradora
valley el valle
vase florero
very muy
very few poquitos
very pretty muy lindo
view vista
violence violencia
violent violento
violin el violín
vocabulary vocabulario
voice la voz
volleyball el vóleibol
vote voto
waiter mesero
waitress mesera
wallet cartera
war guerra
washbasin lavabo
washer la lavadora
watch el reloj
water el agua

wave ola
we nosotros, nosotras
weak débil
weapon el arma
weather tiempo, el clima
wedding boda
Wednesday miércoles
week semana
welcome bienvenidos
well-mannered educado
What? ¿Qué?
When? ¿Cuándo?
Where? ¿Dónde?, ¿Adónde?
Which? ¿Cuál?
white blanco
Who? ¿Quién?
Why? ¿Por qué?
wide ancho
wife esposa
wild salvaje
window ventana
wine vino
wine and fruit juice sangría
winter invierno
wire el alambre
with con
with me conmigo
with you (*between friends, family*) contigo
with him/her/them consigo
without sin
woman la mujer
wood madera
word palabra
work trabajo
world mundo
writer el escritor
written escrito
wrong equivocado
yard patio
year año
yellow amarillo
yes sí
yesterday ayer
yet todavía, aún
you (*between friends and family*) tú
you usted
you guys ustedes
young jóven
young man el jóven
younger menor
your (*between friends and family*) tu
your su
yours suyo
yours (*between friends and family*) tuyo
zebra cebra
zero cero
zip code zona postal
zoo zoológico

Spanish—English

a to
a lo largo de along
a veces sometimes
abajo downward
abeja bee
abierto open
abogado lawyer
abrazo hug
abrigo overcoat
abril April
abuela grandmother
abuelo grandfather
aburrido bored
acá here
acción, la action
aceite, el oil
acera sidewalk
acerca de about
acondicionador, el
  air conditioner
acostarse lie down
actríz, la actress
adelante ahead, forward
además besides
adentro inside
adherir to stick
adiós good-bye
adivinar guess
¿Adónde? Where?
aduana customs
aeropuerto airport
afuera outside
afueras, las outskirts
agencia agency
agencia de viajes travel
  agency
agosto August
agradable pleasant
agrio sour
agua, el water
aguja needle
ahí there
ahora nowadays
ahora mismo right now
ahorrar save
aire acondicionado, el air
  conditioning
ajedrez, el chess

ajo garlic
al to the
al revés backward
alambre, el wire
alfiler, el pin
alfombra rug
alguien someone
algún, algunos, algunas
  some
alicates, los pliers
alma, el soul
almohada pillow
alrededor (de) around
alto tall
allá over there
amante, el lover
amar to love
amargo bitter
amarillo yellow
ambos both
americano American
amigo friend
amistoso friendly
amor, el love
anaranjado orange (color)
ancho wide
ancioso anxious
ángel, el angel
anillo ring
animal, el animal
aniversario anniversary
anoche last night
anochecer, el dusk
anteayer day before yesterday
antes before
anuncio announcement
año year
aparato estereofónico stereo
apartamento apartment
apasionado passionate
apellido surname
apenas just
aplicación, la application
aplicado studious
apostar to bet
aprender to learn
aprovechar to take advantage
apuntes, los notations

aquéllas, aquéllos those
  (over there)
aquí here
araña spider
árbol, el tree
arbusto bush
arena sand
arete, el earring
arma, el weapon
arquitecto architect
arreglar to arrange
arriba upward
arroz, el rice
asfalto asphalt
asistente, el assistant
asistir attend
áspero rough
aspiradora vacuum cleaner
astronauta, el astronaut
atleta, el athlete
aún still, yet
autobús, el bus
avenida avenue
avión, el airplane
ayer yesterday
ayudante, el helper
azul blue
azúcar, el sugar
bahía bay
bailar to dance
baile, el dance
bajo short (in height), low
balde, el bucket
baldosa floor tile
banco bank
bandera flag
baño bathroom
barato inexpensive
barco boat
barrio neighborhood
bastante enough
bata de baño bathrobe
batería battery
batido de leche milkshake
básico basic
básquetbol, el basketball
beber to drink
bebé, el baby

bebida drink
beisbol, el baseball
bello beautiful
besar to kiss
beso kiss
Biblia Bible
biblioteca library
bicicleta bicycle
bienvenidos welcome
billón, el billion
bistec, el steak
blanco white
blando soft
blanqueador, el bleach
blusa blouse
boda wedding
bola ball
boleto ticket
boliche, el bowling
bolsa bag, purse
bombero fireman
bonito pretty
bosque, el forest
bota boot
bote de basura, el trash can
botella bottle
botones, el bellboy
boxeo boxing
brazalete, el bracelet
brevemente briefly
brillante bright
broche, el brooch
bueno good
bufanda scarf
buscar look for
caballo horse
cada each
cadena chain
café, el coffee
cafetera coffee pot
caja box (container)
cajero cashier
cajón drawer
calcetines, los socks
caldo broth
calefacción, la heating
calendario calendar
caliente hot

160

calle, la street
calor, el heat
calvo bald
calzoncillos, los shorts
cama bed
cámara camera
camarón, el shrimp
cambio change
camello camel
caminar to walk
camino road
camionero truck driver
camión, el truck
camisa shirt
camiseta T-shirt
campamento campgrounds
campesino farmer
campo field, countryside
cancha court (sport)
cangrejo crab
canica marble (toy)
cansado tired
cantar to sing
cántaro pitcher
cantina bar (drinking)
capítulo chapter
la carcel jail
caricatura cartoon
carne, la meat
carnicería meat market
caro expensive
carpintero carpenter
carretera highway
carro car
carta playing card, letter
    (mail)
cartera wallet
cartón, el cardboard
casa house
casi almost
castigo punishment
católico Catholic
catorce fourteen
cebolla onion
cebra zebra
ceder to yield
celebrar to celebrate
celoso jealous
cementerio cemetery
cemento cement
cenicero ashtray
centro downtown
Centroamérica Central
    America
ceño frown
cepillo brush
cerca near; fence
cerdo pork
cereza cherry
cero zero
cerrado closed
cerradura lock
cerrar to close
cerro hill
cerveza beer
cielo heaven
cien hundred
cientos hundreds
cierto certain
cigarrillo cigarette
cinco five
cincuenta fifty
cine, el movie
cinta ribbon
cinturón, el belt

circo circus
cita appointment
clarinete, el clarinet
claro light (not dark)
clavo nail
cliente, el client
clima, el climate, weather
cobarde, el coward
cobija blanket
cocido cooked
cocina kitchen
cocinar to cook
cocinero chef
código del área area code
coger to catch
cohete, el rocket
collar, el necklace
comedor, el dining room
comida food, meal
compañero buddy
computadora computer
comunidad, la community
comunismo communism
con with
concierto concert
conferencia conference
confiar to trust
conmigo with me
consigo with him/her/them
construir build
contaminación, la pollution
contestar to answer
contigo with you (between
    friends, family)
contra against
contrario opposite
contrato contract
controlar control
conversación, la
    conversation
copiadora copier
corazón, el heart
corbata tie
correctamente correctly
correcto correct
correo mail, post office
correr run
cortar to cut
corte de pelo, el haircut
corte, la court
cortina curtain
corto short (in length)
cosa thing
costa coast
crema cream
criada maid
crimen, el crime
cristiano Christian
crudo raw
cruel mean
cruz cross
cuaderno notebook
cuadra block (city)
¿Cuál? Which?
cualquiera any
cualquiera parte anywhere
cualquiera persona anyone
¿Cuándo? When?
¿Cuánto? How much?
¿Cuántos? How many?
cuarenta forty
cuatro four
Cuba Cuba
cucaracha cockroach
cuchara spoon

cuchillo knife
cuenta bill, account
culpa fault, blame
cumpleaños, el birthday
cuñada sister-in-law
cuñado brother-in-law
cupón, el coupon
champú, el shampoo
chaqueta jacket
cheque, el check
chicle, el gum
chico small
chimenea chimney
China China
chiste, el joke
chistoso funny
chivo goat
chulo cute
dama lady
dar to give
de of, from
de repente suddenly
debajo underneath
débil weak
decir to say
dejar to leave behind; to allow
del of the
delantal, el apron
demasiado too much
democracia democracy
dentista, el dentist
deporte, el sport
derecha right (direction)
desarollar to develop
descansar to rest
descompuesto out of order,
    broken-down
descripción, la description
descuento discount
desde from
desear to wish
desierto desert
desodorante, el deodorant
despacio slowly
después afterwards
destornillador, el
    screwdriver
desván, el attic
desviación, la detour
detergente, el detergent
detrás behind
día, el day
diablo devil
diálogo dialogue
diamante, el diamond
diario daily
dibujar to draw
diccionario dictionary
dieta diet
diez ten
diez y nueve nineteen
diez y ocho eighteen
diez y seis sixteen
diez y siete seventeen
diferente different
difícil difficult
dinero money
Dios God
dirección, la address
discutir discuss
disponible available
distancia distance
diversión, la fun
divertirse to enjoy oneself
doce twelve

dólar, el dollar
dolor, el pain
doméstico domestic
domingo Sunday
¿Dónde? Where?
dormido asleep
dormir to sleep
dos two
droga drug
ducha shower
duda doubt
dueño owner
dulce sweet
dulce, la candy
duro hard (to touch)
edificio building
educado well-mannered
efectivamente effectively
ejemplo example
ejercicio exercise
él he, him
el the (m., sing.)
electricidad, la electricity
eléctrico electric
elefante, el elephant
elegante elegant
elevador, el elevator
ella she, her
ellos, ellas they
embarasada pregnant
emergencia emergency
empezar to begin
empleado employee
empujar to push
en at, in, on
encima above
encontrar to find
enchufe, el outlet
enemigo enemy
enero January
enfermedad, la sickness
enfermera nurse
enfrente de in front of
enganche, el down payment
enojado angry
ensalada salad
entonces then
entrada entrance
entre between
entrenador, el coach
entrenamiento training
entrevista interview
equipo team
equivocado wrong
esa, ese that
ésa, ése that one
esas, esos those
ésas, ésos those (there)
escalera ladder
escaleras, las stairs
escoba broom
escribir a máquina to type
escrito written
escritor, el writer
escritorio desk
escuchar to listen
escuela school
eso that
España Spain
español Spanish
especial special
espejo mirror
esperanza hope
esposa wife
esposo husband

esquiar ski
esquina, la corner
esta, este this
ésta, éste this one
estación, la season; station
estacionamiento, el parking
estacionar to park
estadio stadium
Estados Unidos United States
estar to be (*location and condition*)
estas, estos these
éstas, éstos these ones
este east
esto this
estrecho narrow
estructura structure
estudiante, el student
estudio study
estufa stove
estúpido stupid
evitar to avoid
examen, el test
excelente excellent
excusado toilet
experiencia experience
extraño strange
fábrica factory
fácil easy
falda skirt
falta fault
faltar to miss
familia family
famoso famous
fantasma, el ghost
fantástico fantastic
farmacia pharmacy
favorito favorite
fé, la faith
febrero February
fecha date
felicitaciones congratulations
fiel faithful
fiesta party
filosofía philosophy
fin, el end
finalmente finally, at last
finca farm
flaco thin
flor, la flower
florero vase
flotar to float
fondo bottom
forma form
fósforo match
fotografía photograph, photography
Francia France
frasco jar
frase, la sentence
fresa strawberry
fresco fresh
frío cold
frito fried
frontera border
fuegos artificiales fireworks
fuerte strong
fumar smoke
furioso furious
fútbol, el soccer
gabinete, el cabinet
galleta cookie
gancho hanger
ganga bargain
garaje, el garage

garganta throat
gasolinera gas station
gastar spend
gato cat
gemelo twin
gente, la people
gerente, el manager
gimnasio gymnasium
globo balloon
gobierno government
golpear to hit
goma rubber
gordo fat
gorra cap
gracias thanks
gramática grammar
grande big, large
gringo American
gris gray
gritar to yell
guante, el glove
guapo handsome
guerra war
guía, el/la guide
guisante, el pea
guitarra guitar
habitación, la room
hablar to speak
hacer to do, to make
hacer una llamada to make a call
hacia towards
hambre, el hunger
hamburguesa hamburger
hasta until
hay there is, there are
helado ice cream
helicóptero helicopter
hermana sister
hermano brother
hermoso lovely
herramienta tool
hielo ice
hija daughter
hijo son
hilo thread
hipopótamo hippopotamus
hispánico Hispanic
hispano Hispanic
hoja leaf, sheet (*paper*)
hola hello
hombre, el man
honesto honest
hora time (*hour*)
horario schedule
hormiga ant
hospital, el hospital
hoy today
huelga strike
huevo egg
humo smoke
idioma language; tongue
iglesia church
igualmente likewise, same to you
impermeable, el raincoat
importancia importance
importante important
incorrecto incorrect
infierno hell
información, la information
ingeniero engineer
Inglaterra England
inglés English
inmediatamente immediately

insecto insect
instrumento instrument
inteligente intelligent
interesante interesting
introducción, la introduction
invierno winter
isla island
izquierda left (*direction*)
jabón, el soap
jalar to pull
jamón, el ham
Japón, el Japan
jardín, el garden
jardinero gardener
jefe, el boss
Jesucristo Jesus Christ
jirafa giraffe
joya jewel
joyería jewelery shop
jóven young, young man
judía verde grean bean
judío Jew
juego game
juego de damas checkers
jueves Thursday
jugar to play (*a game*)
jugo juice
julio July
junio June
junta meeting
juntar to join
juntos together
justicia justice
kilogramo kilogram (*2.2 pounds*)
kilómetro kilometer (*5/8 of a mile*)
la, las the (*f.*)
lado side
ladrillo brick
ladrón, el thief
lago lake
lágrima tear (*crying*)
lámpara lamp
langosta lobster
lanzar to pitch, to cast
lápiz pencil
largo long
lata can
latino Latin
lavabo washbasin
lavadora washer
lavandería laundromat
lavar to wash
lección, la lesson
lectura reading
leche, la milk
lechuga lettuce
leer to read
lejos far
lengua tongue, language
lento slow
león, el lion
letra letter (*alphabet*)
levantarse to raise oneself up
ley, la law
librero bookcase
libro book
licencia de chófer driver's license
licuadora blender
limón, el lemon
limonada lemonade
limpio clean
lista list

listo ready; clever
litro liter
loco crazy
lodo mud
los the (*m., pl.*)
lote de carro, el car lot
luego later
lugar, el place, site
lunes Monday
luz, la light
llanta tire (*auto*)
llave, la key
llegar to arrive
lleno full
llevar to carry
llorar to cry
lluvia rain
madera wood
madre mother
madrugada dawn
maduro ripe
maestro teacher
magia magic
magnífico magnificent
maíz, el corn
maleta suitcase
maletín, el briefcase
mancha stain
mandato command
manera manner
manguera hose
mano, la hand
mantel, el tablecloth
mantequilla butter
manzana apple
mañana tomorrow
mapa, el map
maquillaje, el makeup
máquina de escribir typewriter
mar, el sea
maravilloso marvelous
marea tide
martes Tuesday
martillo hammer
marzo March
más more
matrimonio marriage
mayo May
mayor older
mayoría majority
mayúscula capital (*letter*)
máximo maximum
mecánico mechanic
mediano medium
medianoche midnight
medicina medicine
médico doctor
medio half, middle
mediodía, el noon
menor younger
menos less
mentira lie (*not true*)
mes, el month
mesa table
mesera waitress
mesero waiter
método method
metro (*abr. for metropolitano*) meter, subway
México Mexico
mi, mis my
miedo fear
miel, la honey

miembro member
mientras during
miércoles Wednesday
mil thousand
milagro miracle
millonario millionaire
millón, el million
minoría minority
minúscula lowercase (*letter*)
minuto minute
mío, mía mine
mirar to watch
mismo same
mitad, la half
mochila knapsack
moderno modern
momento moment
moneda coin
mono monkey
montar to ride (*on the back of an animal*)
montar a caballo horseback riding
morado purple
moreno dark-haired
mosca fly (*insect*)
mostaza mustard
mostrar to show
motocicleta motorcycle
motor, el engine
mucho a lot (*much*)
muchos a lot (*many*)
mueblería furniture store
muebles, los furniture
muerte, la death
muerto dead
mujer, la woman
mundo world
muñeca doll
museo museum
música music
músico musician
muy very
muy lindo very pretty
nacimiento birth
nación, la nation
nacionalidad, la nationality
nada nothing
nadar to swim
nadie no one
naranja orange (*fruit*)
naturaleza nature
navaja razor
navegar sail
Navidad, la Christmas
neblina fog
necesario necessary
negro black
nervioso nervous
nieta, nieto grandchild
nieve, la snow
ninguna, ninguno none
niña, niño child
nombre, el name
Norteamérica North America
norteamericano American (U.S.)
nosotras, nosotros we
nota note
noticias, las news
notificación, la notice
novecientos nine hundred
noventa ninety
novia girlfriend, bride
noviembre November

novio boyfriend, fiancé, groom
novios, los sweethearts
nube, la cloud
nudo knot
nuera daughter-in-law
nuestra(s), nuestro(s) our
nueve nine
nuez, la nut (*food*)
número number
número de teléfono phone number
nunca never
o or
obstruir to block
obvio obvious
océano ocean
octubre October
ochenta eighty
ocho eight
odiar to hate
oferta offer
oficina office
ola wave
olvidar forget
olla pot
once eleven
operación, la operation
ordenar to order
orgulloso proud
oro gold
oscuro dark
oso bear (*animal*)
otoño fall (*season*)
otra, otro another
otra vez again
oveja sheep
padre, el father
padres, los parents
pagar to pay
página page
pago payment
pájaro bird
pala shovel
palabra word
palo stick
pan, el bread
panadería bakery
pandilla gang
pantalones, los pants
pantúflas, las slippers
pañuelo handkerchief
papa potato
papalote, el kite
papel, el paper
par pair, couple
para for
parada de autobús bus stop
paraguas, el umbrella
pardo brown
pareja couple, pair
pariente, el relative
parque, el park
partido political party
pasado past
pasaporte, el passport
pasar to pass, to happen
pasillo hallway
paso step
pastel, el pie
pasto grass
patata potato
patinar to skate
patines, los skates
patio yard

patio de recreo playground
pato duck
pavo turkey
payaso clown
paz, la peace
pegar to hit, to stick
peinarse to comb one's hair
peine, el comb
peligroso dangerous
pelirrojo red-headed
pelota ball
peluquería barber shop
perder to lose
perdido lost
perezoso lazy
perfectamente perfectly
perfume, el perfume
periódico newspaper
perla pearl
pero but
perro dog
perro caliente hot dog
persona person
pesadilla nightmare
pesar to weigh
pescado fish (*cooked*)
pescador, el fisherman
pescar to fish
pez, el fish
picante hot (*spicy*)
piedra stone
pimienta pepper
pintor, el painter
pintura paint
piscina swimming pool
piso floor
piyama pajamas
pizarrón blackboard
placa license plate
plancha iron
planta plant
plantar to plant
plástico plastic
plata silver
plátano banana
platicar to chat
plato plate
pleito fight
plomero plumber
pluma feather; pen
pobre poor
pobreza poverty
poco a little bit
pocos few
podrido rotten
policía police (*force* and *person*)
política politics
póliza policy
polvo dust
pollo chicken
poner to put
poquito a very little bit
poquitos very few
por for
por algún lugar somewhere
por eso therefore
por favor please
por fin at last, finally
por ningún lado nowhere
¿Por qué? Why?
por todas partes everywhere
porque because
portón, el gate
posesión, la possession

posible possible
postre, el dessert
práctica practice
precio price
precioso precious
pregunta question
presentación, la presentation; introduction
presidente, el president
prestar to lend
pretender to court someone
primavera spring
primer, primero, primera first
primo cousin
probar try
problema, el problem
producto product
profesional professional
programa, el program
promesa promise
pronto soon
pronunciación, la pronunciation
propina tip
próximo next
público public
pueblo town
puente, el bridge
puerco pig
puerta door
puesta del sol sunset
punta point
punto dot
que that
¿Qué? What?
quebrar to break
querido darling
queso cheese
¿Quién? Who?
quince fifteen
quinientos five hundred
quitar to take away
rama branch
rancho ranch
rápidamente quickly
rápido quick
raqueta racket
rascacielos, el skyscraper
rastrillo rake
rata rat
rato awhile
ratón, el mouse
razón, la reason
recado message
recámara bedroom
receta recipe
recibir to receive
recibo receipt
recreo recreation
red, la net
refresco refreshment
refrigerador, el refrigerator
reina queen
religión, la religion
reloj, el clock, watch
renunciar to quit
reparación, la repair
reparar to fix
repaso review
repollo cabbage
reservación, la reservation
respeto respect
restaurante, el restaurant
revisar to check

revista magazine
rey, el king
rico rich
rinoceronte, el rhinoceros
río river
risa laughter
roca rock
rojo red
romántico romantic
rompecabezas, el puzzle
ropa clothing
ropa interior underwear
ropero closet
roto broken
rubio blond
sábado Saturday
sábana sheet *(bed)*
sabor, el flavor
saco sports coat
sal, la salt
sala living room
salado salty
salchicha sausage
salida exit
salir to leave, to exit
salsa sauce
salud, la health
salvaje wild
sangría sangria, wine and
   fruit juice
sanitario restroom
santo saint; holy
sartén, la frying pan
saxófono, el saxofón
   saxophone
se alquila for rent
se vende for sale
secadora dryer
seco dry
secretaria secretary
sed, la thirst
segundo second
seguro sure
seguro de auto auto
   insurance
seguro social social security
seis six
selva jungle
sello stamp
semáforo signal light
semana week
semilla seed
sentarse to sit down
señal, la road sign
señor, el mister, man
señora lady
señorita miss, young lady
septiembre September
ser to be
serrucho saw
servilleta napkin

sesenta sixty
setecientos seven hundred
setenta seventy
sexo sex
si if
sí yes
SIDA, el AIDS
siempre always
siete seven
significado meaning
siguiente following, next
silla chair
sillón, el easy chair
símbolo symbol
simpático nice
sin without
sin embargo however,
   nevertheless
sinceramente sincerely
sincero sincere
sitio site, place
sobre over, envelope
sobrevivir survive
sofá, el couch
soldado soldier
sola, solo alone
sólo only
soltero single
sombrero hat
sonido sound
sonrisa smile
soñar to dream
soñoliento sleepy
sopa soup
sorprendido surprised
sótano basement
Sr. *(abr. for* **señor)** Mr.
Sra. *(abr. for* **señora)** Mrs.
Srta. *(abr. for* **señorita)** Miss
su your; his; her; their
suave smooth
sube y baja, el seesaw
subir to climb
suceder to happen
sucio dirty
Sudamérica South America
suegro, el father-in-law
sueño dream
suerte, la luck
suéter, el sweater
supermercado supermarket
suyo his, hers, yours, theirs
tamaño, el size
también too, also
tambor, el drum
tampoco neither
tan so
tarde late
tarea homework
tarjeta de crédito credit card
tarjeta postal postcard

taza cup
té, el tea
tela cloth
teléfono telephone
televisión, la television
televisor, el television
tema, el theme
temprano early
tenedor, el fork
tener to have
tenis, el tennis
terminar to finish
terrible terrible
terrífico terrific
tesoro treasure
tía aunt
tío uncle
tiempo time; weather
tienda store
tierra dirt
tigre, el tiger
tijeras, las scissors
timbre, el doorbell
tímido shy
tina bathtub
tirar to throw, to cast
tiza chalk
toalla towel
tocador, el dresser
tocar to touch; to play *(an
   instrument)*
todavía yet
todo all
todo el mundo everybody
todos everybody
todos los días every day
tomar take; drink
tonto dumb
tornillo screw
toronja grapefruit
torta cake
tostador, el toaster
trabajar to work
trabajo work, job
traducir to translate
traer to bring
tráfico traffic
traje, el suit
traje de baño, el swimsuit
traje de entrenamiento, el
   sweatsuit
trapeador, el mop
traste, el dish
trece thirteen
treinta thirty
tren, el train
tres three
tú you *(between friends and
   family)*
tu your *(between friends and
   family)*

tubería plumbing
turista, el/la tourist
tuyo yours
último last
una vez once
una, un a
unas, unos some
universidad, la university
uno one
usted you
ustedes you guys
usualmente usually
uva grape
vaca cow
vacación, la vacation
vacío empty
valiente brave
valle, el valley
varios several
vaso glass *(drinking)*
veinte twenty
venado deer
vendedor, el
   salesperson
vender to sell
venta sale
ventana window
verano summer
verdad, la truth
verde green
vestido dress
vestirse to get dressed
viajar to travel
víbora snake
vida life
vidrio glass
viejo old
viernes Friday
vino wine
violencia violence
violento violent
violín, el violin
visitar to visit
vista view
vocabulario vocabulary
volar to fly
vóleibol, el volleyball
volver to return
voto vote
voz, la voice
y and
ya already
yerno son-in-law
yo I
zanahoria carrot
zapatería shoe store
zapato shoe
zona postal zip code
zoológico zoo

Personal Success Chart

Date   *Mi experiencia*

_____

I used a greeting!

_____

Understood my Spanish-speaking neighbor!

_____

_____

_____

_____

_____